WITNESS AT THE GATES OF HEAVEN

Witnessing God's Mercy as a Hospice Nurse

DENISE D PARKER

Denise D Parker (signature)

WestBow Press
A DIVISION OF THOMAS NELSON
& ZONDERVAN

Copyright © 2021 Denise D Parker.

All rights reserved. No part of this book may be used or reproduced by any means, graphic, electronic, or mechanical, including photocopying, recording, taping or by any information storage retrieval system without the written permission of the author except in the case of brief quotations embodied in critical articles and reviews.

This book is a work of non-fiction. Unless otherwise noted, the author and the publisher make no explicit guarantees as to the accuracy of the information contained in this book and in some cases, names of people and places have been altered to protect their privacy.

WestBow Press books may be ordered through booksellers or by contacting:

WestBow Press
A Division of Thomas Nelson & Zondervan
1663 Liberty Drive
Bloomington, IN 47403
www.westbowpress.com
844-714-3454

Because of the dynamic nature of the Internet, any web addresses or links contained in this book may have changed since publication and may no longer be valid. The views expressed in this work are solely those of the author and do not necessarily reflect the views of the publisher, and the publisher hereby disclaims any responsibility for them.

Any people depicted in stock imagery provided by Getty Images are models, and such images are being used for illustrative purposes only.
Certain stock imagery © Getty Images.

Unless otherwise indicated, all Scripture taken from the New King James Version®. Copyright © 1982 by Thomas Nelson. Used by permission. All rights reserved.

Scripture marked (KJV) taken from the King James Version of the Bible.

ISBN: 978-1-6642-4481-8 (sc)
ISBN: 978-1-6642-4480-1 (hc)
ISBN: 978-1-6642-4482-5 (e)

Library of Congress Control Number: 2021918798

Print information available on the last page.

WestBow Press rev. date: 9/28/2021

DEDICATION

I am dedicating this book to every precious soul I had the honor of serving during my time as a hospice nurse. And to each of their loving family members, who opened their hearts and their homes to me. You will always be treasured in my heart.

EPIGRAPH

For we are to God the fragrance of Christ among those who are being saved and among those who are perishing. (2 Corinthians 2:15)

CONTENTS

Dedication v
Epigraph vii
Preface xi
Acknowledgments xiii

Cold Reality 1
A Seed Is Planted 3
Nurturing the Dream 5
One in Christ 14
Experiencing Childbirth 18
"Mrs. Parker, Jon's Been Injured" 22
Tender Loving Care 27
College at Forty 32
The Wonders of Creation 34
Closer to The White Cap 37
The Call to Arms 39
My Calling Revealed 42
A Joyous Blessing 45
Nightingale's Lamp 47
Thankfully Hired 52

Welcomed to Hospice 58
My Own Caseload 61
They Did Not See Me 66
"I'm an Agnostic" 68
The Heart of Our Father 72
Slipping Away 75
In His Time 79
No Good-Bye 82
On Holy Ground 85
A Slower Pace 87
I Call Her Angel 90
A Sudden End 94
Another Type of Nursing 98
I Will Not Fear 100
Beyond the Gates 105

Bibliography 109

PREFACE

I wrote this book to share the joy and peace I found as I discovered through serving as a hospice nurse, the everlasting love of our Father God. He truly is "not willing that any should perish but that all should come to repentance." (2 Peter 3:9b)

Seeing His interaction with those so close to the gates of heaven, increased my faith, and gave me the assurance that He is a good, good Father. I pray that this account serves to encourage all those who may be close to those same gates, or love someone who is. I pray also for those grieving someone who has passed through those very gates, that they may trust our loving Father with the lives of their loved ones.

ACKNOWLEDGMENTS

I would like to acknowledge all of those who supported, encouraged, and prayed for me as I sought to follow God's calling into hospice nursing: my husband Dennis Parker, my children, Lisa Parker and Jonathan Parker, and my good friends, Gretchen Whitaker, and Beverly A. Hebler.

My heartfelt thanks to all of those saints who worked alongside me, as we cared for those so close to heaven. I'm so grateful for all of my fellow nurses, social workers, home health aides, facility staff, and volunteers, who gave their hearts to the tender care of our patients and their families.

My sincere thanks to every one of you, and God bless you all, for being His angels on earth.

COLD REALITY

It was a cold winter morning in November. Ice was on the ground, and I had pulled up next to the trailer home where my patient was waiting for my visit. I didn't want to go in. I was overwhelmed with the gravity of my job. The job I loved, the job I'd dreamed of having all my life.

Just too much had happened to me in the past year– the sudden loss of my brother in a tragic accident, and the fragile state of my mental health following the discovery of dark family secrets. My shield of strength that had always protected me from the horrors of my job was crumbling away. I was vulnerable, feeling too much sadness to be able to bear it any longer. My body was sore and feeling the effects of age and excess weight, and I wept. I prayed for help, asking God to save me from having to continue in the job I had treasured with all my heart. It took a while for me to dry my tears and to be able to go in and see the sweet lady who depended on me to provide her nursing care. I walked cautiously over the ice that covered the walkway leading to her front door. She welcomed me in, and after asking how she was feeling, I leaned forward to put my stethoscope over her heart while she was seated in her recliner. It was only a slight bending over; I could not comprehend what it did to me! It felt as if a bolt of lightning had struck my spine, sending excruciating pain, like fire, all the way down from my back, to my leg, and down to my foot in an instant! She could not see my face from her position, and I dared not move, frozen in pain beyond belief. My mind was racing! I had never had any signs or symptoms of back problems, and I was always strong and able to reposition my patients with no trouble. I could not let her know; I was there to help and encourage her. She had become quite attached to me, and she would be upset if she knew. It took everything in me to even speak; the pain was all-encompassing. Finally, I braced myself on the arm of her chair to stand up straight. I told her my visit had to be short due to an urgent call, and I managed to make my way to the car without collapsing or slipping on the ice. I called my boss and told her. That would be the last visit I would make as a hospice case managing RN.

A SEED IS PLANTED

I was about five years old when my doctor determined that I should have my tonsils removed. Quite a common surgery when I was young. I remember so clearly the long halls of the hospital and the kindness of the nurse who cared for me. I don't know why she took such an interest in me. I don't remember being afraid, but I must have been full of questions, because this angel in white proceeded to take me on a grand tour of the hospital. She explained the purpose of each area, showing me the equipment in different departments and even introduced me to other young patients, telling me how hospital staff would be helping them. Then she took me to the operating room, and explained how the doctor would remove my tonsils. She told me they would be putting me to sleep first so I would not feel a thing. I was happy that I would get to sleep; I loved sleeping! I remember her dressing me and walking along side me as they wheeled me into the operating room. Then they put me to sleep, and during surgery, I dreamed that the doctor used one of those long, skinny, plasticware teaspoons from the fifties, slipping it down my throat, and scooped out my tonsils. When I woke up, I really thought that was how he had removed them! It didn't hurt as bad as I'd thought it would. I loved the ice chips and ice cream. But more than all that, I had fallen head over heels in love with nursing! I wanted that white uniform with the perky white cap, white stockings, and white shoes that hardly made any sound at all! I drew a large picture of myself as a nurse when I was a bit older. Hating my red hair due to the teasing, I drew myself as a brunette. Momma said sometimes your hair changes color as you grow up, and I was hopeful I would grow out of my red hair. But I never did grow out of it or my desire to become a nurse!

> Delight yourself also in the LORD,
> And He shall give you the desires of your heart.
> Commit your way to the LORD, Trust also in Him,
> And He shall bring it to pass. (Psalm 37:4–5)

NURTURING THE DREAM

The human body always fascinated me! When I was quite young, Momma and I were on the bus, and we saw a man sitting behind us with his arm up. One of his hands was propped by a circular metal frame connected to a metal band around his wrist. Each damaged finger was held in place by wires connected to the frame. It was a serious injury, something no one on the bus would look at. I could not stop looking at it; I was mesmerized, staring in wonderment. My mother gently told me that it was not polite to stare. And she explained that he must have been injured, and this would help him. Although I was quite young, I was not disturbed; I was only fascinated by what I was seeing.

There was a television show I loved to watch that showed surgeries. I can't imagine what that show could have been. It was in the early sixties. I remembered my mom didn't want to see it, and she questioned my rapt attention to it.

When Christmas came, I was thrilled to get the one thing I really had my heart set on– a Disney Pollyanna doll! Being a walker doll, she was almost life-sized, and I determined that she needed her appendix out. Using the toy nurse's bag was not nearly as satisfying as using a real sewing needle to "cut" (scratch) a line onto her right lower abdomen and then to make stitch marks along the line when I had finished the "operation!" She would eventually have several other "scars" from my care.

When my baby brother was born, I became the protective big sister. He was constantly getting injuries from his reckless exploration. I loved him so! When he was injured, I cried as if I was the one hurt. Once, when I was holding him, he suddenly lurched away from me, and I broke my wrist as I caught him just before he hit the ground! I felt quite proud that I had "saved" him. It was well worth a broken wrist. Later, when he was about three, he became very sick and was in a feverish coma. The doctor told my mom all the things she must do in hopes of bringing his fever down. I shared a room with my brother, and I watched helplessly as Momma did all the doctor told her to do. He was in a coma for two days, before he finally came around. I hardly slept at all during that time, watching carefully to make sure he was breathing. It was a horrible feeling to see him so sick and to watch Momma doing all she could to save him. We all rejoiced the morning he woke up, as if nothing had ever happened! I wanted to be his protector; I was so determined to keep him safe!

I was, however, not so great at keeping myself safe. It was shortly after his illness when we were playing in the small strip of grass in front of our rented duplex, splashing in the water as

Momma washed her car. I ran from her as she sprayed us and stepped firmly on a broken soda bottle hidden in the grass. It was the bottle base with jagged shards sticking up, and when I saw what I had stepped on, I calmly put that foot across my knee, saying, "Mom, I stepped on some glass." Her eyes widened as she saw that I had hit an artery! She called for Daddy to get a towel, and she wrapped my foot in it and put me in the car. Momma was a fast driver! She often raced in that '56 Chevy with me along. I used to holler, "Faster, Mommy, faster, faster!" She drove fast to the corner emergency clinic. By the time they got me in there, the towel was thoroughly soaked through. After they stitched me up, I was amazed how small the cut was that produced such a fountain. I asked the nurse, and she told me all about what arteries were.

The only time I was truly frightened by a medical emergency happened about a year later. My girlfriend and I were talking to my daddy as he was working on a go-cart he was building. He suddenly began looking into the sky as if he was trying to see something, and then without warning, he hit the ground as if someone had slammed him down. His head hit the bumper of the car parked next to us, and he was injured, thrashing and moaning. I ran screaming for Momma. She told me to go inside and stay there. I thought Daddy was dying! A neighbor came in to calm me, but I could not be consoled. I just knew that Daddy must be dying. It was a long time before Momma brought Daddy in, and he was dazed, not able to talk, and was wandering aimlessly through the house. He finally went to bed and fell into a deep sleep. That was when Momma told me about epilepsy. Daddy had had it since he was a teenager, and his family doc kept it a secret, so that he could still be gainfully employed. Daddy was a carpenter, and was often high up on a building as he framed it. Momma told me how she always worried about when and where the next attack would happen. Daddy took the medicine his doctor gave him, but sometimes he would forget. The next day when I was calmed down, Momma took me to the car and showed me how to stop the car if it should happen while Daddy was driving. Momma also taught me to never put anything in his mouth during a seizure. To only keep watch over him, making sure there is nothing harmful close to him. Daddy slept over twenty-four hours after that seizure. Daddy's seizures were the "Grand mal" type. It was only a short time later that it happened again. Daddy usually had seizures when he was concentrating hard on something. We were moving into our first home, and Daddy was busy trying to install drapery rods in the newly built tract home, while Momma, my brother and baby sister were at our old duplex. I was outside when I heard screaming, and I came running in to find Daddy on the floor, my aunt and uncle with him and they had put a pencil in his mouth! I told them "NO! You can't do that!" And seconds later Daddy had crushed the pencil, but I was able to clear the residue away from him. Our old duplex was a long way from where we were. It took a long time for Momma to get there. It was so hard watching Daddy; he eventually woke up and started walking around not knowing where he was or what was happening. He finally fell asleep, and then I broke down, crying alone in my new bedroom. I think the doctor changed his prescription after that because I never saw him have another seizure. I have witnessed many horrific things in my life, but nothing compares to seeing someone you love injured or in danger.

My first experience in helping others in a crisis happened earlier, on November 22, 1963. We were coming in from the playground as an emergency alarm was sounding, and the teachers were gathering us in our rooms. The speaker in our room was playing a direct, national broadcast telling all about how our President, John F. Kennedy, had been assassinated in Dallas, Texas. Our teacher did not speak, but stood at the front of the room trying hard to keep steady as she wept, overcome with emotion. We were released for our lunch break, and all of the teachers I passed were crying, and walking as if in a trance. I was in fifth grade and my fellow classmates were in shock, and upset because our teachers were upset. We were left to continue the day, coping on our own. In the cafeteria, the staff were visibly shaken, and several children got sick in their lunch trays. The girl who was assigned to clean off the trays ran away crying; so I swiftly went to the table where the trays were wiped down, and took over that task. It did not bother me because I was more concerned about helping in any way I could. I calmly soothed my crying classmates as one by one they returned their trays, many having not eaten at all. I will never forget that day; the solemn, weeping teachers, and the frightened, traumatized children. During the televised funeral procession, my heart and my eyes were fixed on little Carolyn and John-John, his children, so young, and yet standing at attention on their own. I wanted to hold them and comfort them.

When I was eleven years old and we had moved to our new tract home in the suburbs, Momma depended a lot on me. She never really had a stomach for messes. My baby sister woke up from a nap and instead of crying for us, she kept herself busy playing with the contents of her dirty diaper. When Momma went in to check on her, she came out screaming, "I cannot do this!" I spoke up and said, "Don't worry Momma, I will take care of it." I giggled as my sister continued to play, oblivious to the mess she had made in her crib, on the walls, and on every square inch of herself! I nicknamed her "Pooper" that day. I took great pride in cleaning up that mess. Momma was in the bathroom tearful as she was rinsing some of the things as I handed them to her, and taking them to the washing machine. Momma did *not* like messes! She was a perfect housekeeper, keeping every area as clean as possible. Our home was comfortable, but very clean! She often used a pine scented cleaner with a smell that I hated. I could smell it before I even entered the house as I came home from school. I, on the other hand, was far from tidy. Momma tried, but I rejected her immaculate influences. My room was always a mess. Germs did not bother me! So, she left the dirty chores to me; like getting rid of any bugs and burying little pets, like hamsters and fish. I also assumed the cleaning up and nursing of my brother and sister when they were sick or injured. One time my sister really hurt herself in a foolish accident. The neighborhood boys made a small ramp so they could jump their bikes and get some "air." Wanting to be involved, my sister decided to make it more exciting by laying down at the end of the ramp! The first kid to try the jump after she was there, chickened out at the last second and rode his bike right over my sister's face! Mom was beside herself when she saw her. My sister was such a pretty little girl, and now her nose was obviously broken, and quite crooked! I calmly took over for Mom and told her that her nose was broken and she would have to go to the hospital. It turned out her nose was broken, in two places!

I was the one the neighborhood kids would run to when they were injured while playing, and I was happy to patch them up. I seemed to be able to easily take over during those minor emergencies, staying calm, and doing what was needed. That came in handy when I was twelve and started babysitting in the neighborhood. The parents were always happy with my care and the confidence I showed in caring for their children. The money I made was a great way to pay for the records I wanted, and the dresses I wore to school.

In high school, girlfriends would come to me for advice about their personal issues, and word spread around that I was the one to ask for personal advice. After getting my own ears pierced by a neighbor, I carried an ear-piercing kit in my purse, hoping I could pierce someone else's ears! I didn't get that chance until I was eighteen. My girlfriend asked me if I had ever done it before, and I lied, saying I did it all the time. After successfully piercing her ears, she asked, "How many people's ears have you pierced?" Then I told her she was the first! She wasn't too mad, and forgave me quickly because her ears turned out great.

All of my eagerness and desire to become a nurse, did not change the fact that my parents could not afford to send me to college for a nursing degree. I was so hopeful when they built a college a block away from our house, and they had a nursing program! My counselors at school felt I should pursue a career in the arts, and they did not support my desire to become a nurse. After all, I had failed math and had a D in science! I was doing quite well in my Speech class, winning awards in Original Oratory. I loved writing, but I really wanted to wear that white cap and those white stockings! It would be a long time before that dream came true.

My mom bought me a typewriter for my high school graduation party. She was always supportive of my writing. So was my grandpa Wally, who was a lifelong writer, and my encourager. I had sent him a sample of my writing in my first year of high school, asking for his critique. He was kind in his letter back to me, but said that I should buy a better typewriter, because the one I had wouldn't do the job for me! The one Momma bought me was perfect! It was a year after my graduation, when I became engaged to my future husband. Excited for him to meet my grandpa, he went along with me and my mom to visit him. I wanted to personally invite him to our wedding. I knew he had been diagnosed with cancer, but it was a shock seeing him with the scars and disfigurement from his surgery for throat and neck cancer. He was not the perky man I remembered. He was calm and seemed accepting of what he was facing. He gave his blessing to our marriage, welcoming my fiancé to the family. I'm so thankful that Mom took a photo of me and Grandpa together. After I was home alone in my bedroom, I broke down and cried, mourning him, knowing he would be dying soon. It was in June that we saw him, and he passed away in July, several months before our wedding. I did not want to go to the funeral. It was just too hard for me. My mom and uncles all tried to convince me to go, knowing how close I was to him, but I would not. I could not. I knew I would not be physically able to. Because he meant so much to me. It was my first experience of losing a loved one.

And I loved him so much! His battle with cancer was too much for me to handle, and it distanced me from the very thought of nursing. A few months later, we were married, and I became the happy bride of my one true love, Dennis Parker. I buried my dreams of writing or nursing, focusing instead on my real-life dream, as a wife and mother.

In memory of my precious Grandpa Wally; this is the poem he wrote for me on my third birthday:

Ode To Denny

Just a little baby kid
With hair a sunburnt red
"Just a little baby kid"
As I've so often said…
A beautiful little bundle…
Whose heart is full of glee
And in no time at all
She's reached the age of three.
She tries a lot of speech
Picked up from her glamorous "Maw"
But to me her favorite words are
"Mine, mine, mine 'Bop Paw!'"
(Lester Wallace Reed)

ONE IN CHRIST

I discovered quickly that becoming one in Christ, really is becoming one flesh. One cannot be injured or hurt without the other feeling pain. I had bought a Bible bookmark to put in my wedding Bible, with this phrase, "Marriage – Henceforth there shall be such a oneness between you that when one weeps the other will taste salt." (M. Buxbaum) This became very real to me and to Dennis in the first year we were married.

Dennis was visiting his parents when I was returning home from work listening to my radio, speeding along a main road at night, when I approached an intersection. The light had just turned yellow as I approached, so I kept going knowing I could easily make the light. But I did not realize that the driver of the car waiting for the signal, decided to jump the light before it turned green, and was suddenly right in front of me! I slammed on my brakes, and everything went into slow motion, as I saw a woman sitting in the passenger seat a few feet away, right where I was heading! I turned my wheel seconds before impact and hit the front side wheel instead of her passenger seat, and I saw the car spin away from me in slow motion as I came to a sudden stop. All of the force of the impact was on me and my car. My skid marks were only a few feet long before impact, revealing the instantaneous nature of the crash. The other car, a big American car, had spun around and was facing the opposite direction. My car, a small Datsun 510, stopped dead at the site of impact. It threw my body so far forward that I felt my lower body and legs going all the way under the dash, while both hands that had been firmly grasping the steering wheel slipped off and hit the dash as my head hit the window. All in slow motion. I heard the tires screeching, the metal clashing and glass shattering. Suddenly, it was silent. I had always been an avid seatbelt advocate. When Dennis took me on our first date he said, "No one rides in my car without a seatbelt." I was thrilled because I felt the same way. I always wore my seatbelt; but in shock, I thought I couldn't have had it on, or I would not have hit the window or slid so far under the dash! So I pushed open the car door and tried to get out, only to find that I was still buckled tightly in my seatbelt! The impact was so great my entire body flew forward, except for my upper torso, where my trusty seat and chest belts held on tightly. I stumbled out to check the other car, and they were fine, but my car was totaled! It didn't look as if anyone would have survived in that car! On wobbly legs I answered the policemen's questions, who just happened to be across the street on a break and saw it all. Then I made my way, shaking to the corner market to call Dennis. When his mom answered the phone, she said Dennis had already left and was heading home. Just as I came out of the market, I was startled and jumped, as I heard the sound of loud screeching from a car that was passing the scene. As I looked, I realized it was Dennis! He was on his way home and saw my car, a tangled wreck in the street, and no Denise! His tires smoked as he stopped his Roadrunner, then threw it in reverse, backing up swiftly, stopping near where I was. I waved frantically for him, and he was amazed to find I was alive, and relatively uninjured. He ran over to me, eyes wide with amazement, and held me tenderly, whispering, "I love you, I love you!" He was my comforter and consoler all night, holding me close as I writhed in pain from all of the bruises and contusions. I had welts on my chest and lap area where the seatbelts had held me. Both hands were black and blue for weeks; but I was alive! I praise God for His protection! I believe He slowed time for me during the crash, to keep me from embedding my car into the middle of the other car where there was no wheel axil to stop me. It would have killed me, the woman in the passenger seat, and also the driver, no doubt! But God allowed me those few seconds, to turn the steering wheel just enough to save us all! Dennis was beside himself with concern for me, doing all he could to help and comfort me. He was so thankful he had not lost me.

A short time later, it was my turn to comfort my husband, when he came home early from work after he tripped and landed on a large piece of wood that pierced through his calf. His boss sent him to emergency and they removed it, but his pain was excruciating! He tossed and moaned all night, and there was nothing I could do to ease his pain. I wept, hurting deep in my spirit for him, not being able to give him the relief he needed to sleep. I thought of that saying on the bookmark, realizing how true it was. We were one flesh, and all we would ever go through, we would be going through as one, together forever in Christ.

> "For this reason a man shall leave his father and mother and be joined to his wife, and the two shall become one flesh;" so then they are no longer two, but one flesh. (Mark 10:7–8)

EXPERIENCING CHILDBIRTH

For this child I prayed, and the LORD has granted me my petition which I asked of Him. (1 Samuel 1:27)

Before I knew it, we were expecting our first baby! I read all I could about how to prepare, including natural childbirth, and breastfeeding. I was so eager to do everything the best way. I went to childbirth classes hoping Dennis would go with me, but it was too frightening to him, so I went alone. He never liked hospitals, doctors or nurses, and only went in an emergency. I understood, but I was determined to give birth naturally. It didn't turn out quite the way I planned! The doctor was going on vacation, so he scheduled an induction for his convenience. Despite that, I was determined to have as natural a childbirth as I could, and refused any pain medication. I also had an advocate on my side; my childbirth instructor agreed to be there and coach me. Dennis was there at the beginning, but went to the waiting room when the real work began. My coach was right there next to me keeping me focused on my breathing and my focal point, a picture of Jesus, which helped tremendously! I even dared to sit upright with my heels together, to allow a swift passage. (In ages past, they had "birthing chairs," that allowed gravity to do the work.) None of this was encouraged or acknowledged by the doctor or nurses at that time. Natural childbirth was at its very beginning, and not recognized by the medical community. I flew through that delivery, and six hours later I joyfully beheld the wide-open eyes of our daughter, Lisa Christina. The doctor was holding her upside down by her feet, then quickly handed her off to a nurse as he ran to the next patient. My joy would be short, as they determined that I should not see her until my milk came in, considering I had the nerve to say I would be breastfeeding! Breastfeeding was quite frowned upon then. It would be forty-eight, long hours later, before they finally released her into my eager, waiting arms!

I truly feel that childbirth is a natural process, and should not be interfered with, unless there is a true emergency. We still have far to go in that regard. Instead of a personal, joyful experience, the joy has been dampened by technology trying to control a natural process. Too many births in America, are by Caesarian Section. What a shame.

Three years later, we had another child on the way. We were both hoping for a boy, but I wanted to be surprised. When the doctor ordered a new technology, a sonogram, to check baby's size, I told the tech that I didn't want to know if it was a boy or girl. Dennis was disappointed because he really wanted to know! There were great improvements by then, in supporting mothers who sought a natural childbirth. I was happy that the hospital I would be using had special rooms were the mom could be with their newborns! But again, things did not go as planned. Baby was quite big, and caused frequent, false labor. After two false trips to the hospital, I decided I would not go unless I was close to delivery. I had plenty of warning that day, and I should have told Dennis to stay home from work while I was having regular, not very painful contractions. Instead, I urged him to go to his night shift, assuring him I would call if I needed him. The contractions were mild, but ten minutes apart, when I drifted off to sleep. I was awakened by a strong contraction, and when I timed the next one, it was five minutes apart. *Oops!* I thought, and quickly called Dennis. I also called his mother, who planned to watch Lisa when I went into labor, and they lived quite far from us. A half hour drive, at least. Dennis had almost as long of a drive, and by the time they both got there, my contractions were two minutes apart and hard! Well, I wanted to wait until almost delivery! Dennis did *not* want to have the baby in his car! It was an Oldsmobile Cutlass V-8, and Dennis knew how to drive it! The hospital was almost twenty miles away, and thankfully it was the middle of the night, so the freeway was clear. He was going about ninety miles per hour, and as we approached the off-ramp we saw a police car on the other side of the freeway, turning around to come after us! But Dennis was already flying through city streets by then, heading for the hospital. We got there not long before the birth, and we were thrilled to welcome our second child, a healthy boy, Jonathan. Only then did we discover that there was a nurse's strike, without enough nurses to monitor the mother/baby rooms, so they kept him in the nursery between feedings. At least they encouraged my breastfeeding! They brought him to me whenever he was hungry. His sister was overjoyed to meet her little brother, and they became the best of friends. Jonathan was fearless and eager to explore. Soon, our active little boy brought the world of nursing back to mind, as he was sending us to the emergency room for frequent visits. That boy! I learned a lot while he was growing up. Soon I was taking out his stitches myself to avoid another trip the doctor's office. It gave me a great sense of satisfaction, as I nursed his wounds. I didn't realize that he was giving me a preceptorship in emergency nursing.

"MRS. PARKER, JON'S BEEN INJURED"

Jon was fifteen years old when one afternoon, I got a phone call from one of his friends. He sounded upset, saying Jon had hurt himself on his bike. That was nothing new, so I told his friend not to worry. But then his friend said, "You don't understand Mrs. Parker, we had to call an ambulance." Like a flash I ran to the car, but Dennis insisted that he drive. I was frantic, and Dennis was not driving fast enough for me! Good thing, too! I would have gotten in an accident, as determined as I was to get there quickly. As we reached the remote location where he was, the street was crowded with emergency vehicles and firetrucks. I leapt out of the car before Dennis could bring it to a stop, and ran up the hill to where our son was. He was sitting in the dirt, surrounded by paramedics who were trying to get a neck brace on him, but he was combative. (Jonathan was almost six foot tall and all muscle.) He was also having trouble seeing anything due to his head and facial injuries. The policeman told me that he had lost his memory, and had been unconscious for quite a while. I felt the paramedics were not helping because they were not answering Jon's questions, "What happened to me? Why can't I remember anything?" So I got down in front of Jon and calmly told him, "Memory loss is common with a head injury son, and you hit your head pretty hard. They just want to help you, and get you to the hospital." Jon calmed right down, and let them do what was needed to transport him. He told me later that he didn't know who I was, and only knew I was his mother because he heard me tell the policeman that I was. One of the best trauma hospitals in our state was a short distance away, and Dennis drove me there to meet them. They did a CT scan, and found there was no damage to his neck or spine, praise God! But then the trauma doctor told me that he had shattered his right cheek bone, misplaced most of his upper right teeth, and the most concerning injury was his palate. He said Jon's palate had a half inch gap in it, and that would require immediate surgery. Unfortunately, we had PPO medical coverage, and they had an ambulance waiting to take him to their hospital, so the trauma doctor said his hands were tied. I overheard two nurses talking about Jon, and they were worried when they heard that they would be transferring him to the PPO hospital. One said, "Oh that poor boy, they will never fix his face!" After hearing that, I went back to the trauma doctor and asked him to tell me exactly what should be done for my son. He told me that his palate was the most critical injury, and had to be surgically repaired. His cheek would also need surgical repair, and his teeth realigned, along with multiple stitches for the cut to his forehead.

He also needed to be monitored closely due to his severe concussion. So reluctantly, we allowed them to transport our son to the PPO hospital. I called our church and told them what had happened, and they started a prayer chain for Jon's healing. It was the longest, hardest night I had ever been through. The PPO staff seemed more concerned with stitching him up, than pursuing his more serious injuries. It wasn't until morning that we were able to see the ENT surgeon. He was going on about how Jon's cheek bone might be able to be repaired, but it would be a delicate surgery. Then he said, that he felt it would be better to just leave it. "What?" I said, I was furious! Then I demanded, "What about his palate?" "What about it?" He responded. Now I was livid! "He has a half inch fracture in it!" I responded, so upset! I had seen the fracture myself, before they transported him to the PPO. The doctor had shown me, asking Jon to open his mouth so that I could see it, as he told me about his injuries. They had a CT scan showing it! Then, the ENT surgeon said, "Mrs. Parker, come over and see." He told Jon to open his mouth, and there was his palate, completely intact and pink, as good as new! God had heard our prayers and healed my boy!

I still insisted that I wanted his cheek bone repaired, and asked to speak to his boss, the chief surgeon. She came in right away and said yes, they can fix it. But Jon had to see the orthodontist first to realign his teeth. And they could not perform the surgery on his cheek until the swelling went down. My poor boy was swollen beyond recognition. He was in a daze through all the doctor visits, until he saw the orthodontist. They could not give him any pain killers due to his head injury and concussion. They asked me to wait in the lobby. I had managed to keep my composure for over twenty-four hours, but when I heard my son crying out in pain, I finally broke down and wept. When it was over, the nurse came out and called me back to see him. I dried my tears and tried to compose myself. He was sitting calmly in the dental chair, and I asked if he was okay. He calmly said, "Yah, I'm okay Mom." I told him I was afraid he would kill the doctor. Then he smiled a crooked, mishappen smile, and said, "No, but I did break his chair!" And he lifted up his hand still gripping the broken chair arm tightly, to show me, like a well-earned trophy.

It would take a few days before we found out exactly what had happened to our son. Jon could not remember anything. We were actually able to see it happen right before our own eyes, as his friend had been taping him when it happened. He liked jumping his BMX bike and doing tricks in the air. He was quite good at it! The tape showed him going up into the air from a dirt ramp, performing a trick, and then appearing to land smoothly, when the bike and Jon suddenly slammed into the ground. We had to use super, slow-motion to see what had happened. The front neck stem, holding his handlebars and front wheel, snapped in two as he landed, throwing him face first into the ground. He seemed lifeless. His friend threw the video recorder down, and ran to him. They told us they thought he had snapped his neck and was dead. You could hear them crying on the recording, not knowing what to do. After some time, Jon came to, but didn't know who he was, where he was, or what had happened. He was stumbling around, and they were trying to calm him down. They got help from a neighbor nearby, and they called emergency. His friends also told us later that they had shown the tape to the first trauma doctor, and he was amazed that Jon had not broken his neck. We knew God had been merciful to our son.

The PPO surgeon was good on her word, and they did the surgery to repair his cheek. He was one of the first people to receive a titanium transplant. They applied it over his cheekbone to hold it together. Representatives from the company that made it were there to observe the surgery. It was a few months before he looked like himself. And Jon had lost a large portion of his childhood memories. He is in his forties now, and still has occasional flashbacks of that accident, seeing the ground racing up in his face. I am still praising God he was not killed, and that God healed his most critical injury.

> For He shall give His angels charge over you, To keep you in all your ways. In their hands they shall bear you up, Lest you dash your foot against a stone. (Psalm 91:11–12)
>
> O LORD my God, I cried out to You,
> And You healed me. (Psalm 30:2)

TENDER LOVING CARE

It was only a year later, that my sweet grandma became too confused to live alone, the way she had for several years. She had always been independent and quite capable. But she started forgetting to pay her bills, or overpaid others, and she was falling often. Dennis encouraged me to bring her home with us, and after she fell and hit her head, I knew it was time. She was so gracious and sweet, as she agreed calmly when I told her she had to come home with me. I think she was relieved. Her dementia increased daily, and we had visiting nurses and bath aides coming in to monitor her, and to help with her personal care. I was envious of the visiting nurse, with her nursing bag, out in the field, serving those in need. I dreamed of having a job like that.

Soon, Grandma's doctor ordered Hospice care. I never regretted bringing her home. She was always such a large part of my life, and a treasure to my family. We took her with us to every excursion or family gathering before her decline. Now we were determined to help her feel at home, and to provide the best care possible. We all loved her so!

Caring for her was my great privilege, and I felt honored to care for the one who had cared for me so often when I was little. It was hard, not the work of caring for her or her incontinence, that came easily for me; but it was the heartache of her realizing that she needed to be cared for that was so hard. I will never forget the morning I found her sitting in her chair, trying to figure out how to dress herself. All she could manage was to carefully drape a sock over her head. I smiled and gently led her to the bathroom where I had to clean her before dressing her. As I was washing her legs, she looked down at me with tears in her eyes and said, "I'm sorry." "Oh Grandma!" I responded, "It is my honor to care for you, the way you cared for me when I was little, I love you."

That was the difficult thing about dementia, she often had windows of clarity, and realized she could not do the simple things she used to take for granted. I learned a lot just watching her. And I learned so much from the Hospice Nurse who visited her. She gave me the knowledge and the confidence I needed to care properly for her. But some of her symptoms were quite hard to deal with. I realized years later, that she had Lewy Body Dementia. It can cause visual hallucinations and delusions. One time she became frightened as she saw snakes covering the floor, and she screamed at me, asking how I could bring her into a house covered with snakes? I tried telling her she was safe and there were no snakes, but she could not be convinced. I got upset trying to convince her, and my son called me outside. He calmly told me, "Mom, that's not Grandma, it's her sickness. She doesn't know what is happening." His words calmed my heart, and I knew he was right. I went back in the house, and just sat with her, my arms around her, until she had calmed down.

Most of the time, she was her own sweet self. She was often clear minded enough to tell me about her life on the farm when she was a little girl, and the time she felt led to go forward in church, and accept Jesus Christ as her Savior. I treasure and remember every word. She meant so much to me, I had to do my best to give her the best care possible. And I didn't mind the physical care giving. It was as soothing for me as it was for her when I bathed her, dressed her, and helped her eat. It broke my heart when I saw her gripping her fork tightly, not being able to make it do what she wanted it to. I switched to finger foods for her then. Slowly, steadily, she declined. Finally, one morning, I went in to find she had a stroke and she could not respond. She just stared at me, frightened. The paramedics took her to the hospital, and my uncles and my mom arrived because the doctor said she was close to dying. They decided to place her in a full care facility, and I was broken hearted. I did not want to lose her! But, lose her I did. She went home to Jesus a few months later, the day before my birthday.

The year I spent caring for her, was a time of personal discovery; as I realized how much I loved care giving. From my brother and sister, to our children, including our adventurous son, who was known by name at the emergency room, to my precious Grandma, I loved every minute of caring for them.

When Jonathan was young, I was overwhelmed with his constant need to try new, adventurous things, and I asked my grandma, how she managed to care for all her children, including three sons. She giggled and told me, that as each child came along, the older ones would help with the younger ones, keeping an eye out for them. I was amazed at the calm, easy going response of a mother and grandmother who had been through so much. Her answer only gave me more respect for her. I would have to learn on my own how to deal with the injuries my son would experience. There were so many! His desire to seek physical thrills led to tree climbing, which advanced to rock climbing, and then his biking, with routine injuries. He had a high pain tolerance, and took it all in stride. Even a short time after his head injury, he was back at the race track, rode around the track, and did a "no-footer" over the double jumps! Yes, my heart was in my throat as I watched him.

He had grown a bit calmer by the time Grandma left us. He was eighteen years old, and I had been thinking a lot about going to college to become an R.N. All I had experienced in my life, was leading to that. My sweet husband knew that it was a lifelong dream of mine, and had encouraged me to pursue it. My daughter, who was married then, also encouraged me. But I had spent the last twenty-four years of my life as a happy homemaker. I never went to college, and the idea of stepping away from my cozy nest and homemaking role, was a bit frightening. But God was whispering to my heart, and I saw an advertisement in our local paper about a college near us that was presenting an introduction to their nursing program. I really wanted to go, but fear was holding me back. So I decided to ask my son, because I felt he would be missing his mom being there for him at home. I told him about the nursing program, and that I was thinking about it, but I didn't want to abandon him. He laughed, and said, "Ma, you need to quit worrying about us, and get on with your life." I did not expect that! I was secretly hoping he would tell me to stay at home. Now, I had no excuse, except to step forward into the path that God had laid out for me.

> Now He who has prepared us for this very thing is God, who also has given us the Spirit as a guarantee. (2 Corinthians 5:5)

COLLEGE AT FORTY

The nursing program would require quite a few college courses before being accepted into the program. I was going to be taking an entrance exam in a week, and I was concerned about math, my most hated subject! So I used a text book that I had used while homeschooling our children. It was a great text, leading you from the beginning of basic math, to Algebra, consecutively. I crammed every bit of information I could into my head until I felt confident enough to take the exam. When I went to the college campus that first time, I got choked up thinking about how long it took for me to get there. But I had such peace about it! I was not nervous or concerned. I trusted that God had led me there for a reason, and I knew He was with me. Indeed, He was! I scored quite high on the entrance exam, which meant I would only have to take one semester of Algebra as a part of my prerequisites. I was thrilled! I was also excited to be taking a full range of courses, eager to learn as much as I could! I would never have had the desire to learn those things when I was 18. All I wanted from high school was the diploma. I got it by the skin of my teeth! I never studied, put my books in my locker when I got them, and when the semester was over, I went to the office to find out what my locker combination was, so I could return the books. I bluffed my way through all four years of high school. There would be no bluffing now! I had my eyes on that nursing degree, and I was determined to be the best student possible.

It was interesting, being the age of some of my classmate's mothers. But age gave me the advantage of understanding that each instructor would have their own style of teaching, and you had to adapt. This was not the place for complaining, but calm acceptance. I was on a steady course, my eyes on the prize, so eager for that white cap!

THE WONDERS OF CREATION

My first nursing course was Anatomy. I always had a thirst for knowledge about our bodies. I was careful to read every new medical discovery in the newspaper, so fascinated by it. Now, I would be learning hands on, and I could hardly wait! I took my studies very seriously, carrying flash cards I had made with me everywhere. I studied every waking moment, and my sweet husband soon asked me how to run the washing machine, so he could have clean clothes to wear. He was so supportive, and never complained, as I buried myself in study. I couldn't help it. It was all so amazing! I developed favorite anatomy parts, like the Arrector Pili muscle. It's one of the smallest muscles, the muscle that contracts to cause "Goose Bumps!" My favorite organ was the kidney, due to the intricacies of its function, until I discovered even more in my Physiology class. That was when the heart became my very favorite organ.

Our instructor, a very wise, calm, intense man, explained that scientists had taken a small scraping of cardiac cells and grew it in a Petri dish, and the cells began to beat! Not in rhythm, but beating just the same. He explained that cardiac tissue was exclusive to the heart, and only it would respond that way. What a glorious Creator we have! At the last class of the semester, he did something awe inspiring, that I will never forget. He had us all meet in the Lecture Auditorium where he separated out DNA, using a centrifuge machine. Before our eyes, he drew up a long, stretchy, thick stand of DNA on a glass rod, stretching it almost two feet from the container! Knowing how small DNA was, and seeing a mass of it, as a thick strand being stretched up like that, seemed impossible. And so wonderful! I was awe struck. But I was also amazed at the lack of interest in many of the young students. They were seeing the stuff of creation, gathered in a visible strand! But it seemed I was the only one who understood the significance of what we had just seen. The professor made eye contact with me, as I gazed in wonder, my eyes and mouth wide open. He knew he had amazed at least one of his students.

Microbiology was another amazing class. I was giddy as I saw the wonders of God's intricate design through the lens of the microscope. The instructor couldn't help but smile and laugh at my enthusiasm and excitement with each new discovery. Oh, the wonders and infinite beauty of His creation! Those classes fed my love for the One who created the heavens and the earth, and cared enough to create all of the beautiful intricacies of our bodies, down to the smallest atom! It seems to be a perfectly conducted orchestra, bringing together millions of elements to create the perfect masterpiece, a human being. What a magnificent creation!

> I will praise You, for I am fearfully and wonderfully made;
> Marvelous are Your works, And that my soul knows very well. (Psalm 139:14)

How sad that we chose rebellion, and sin entered in to our world, bringing with it sickness and death. But it was because of sickness and death, that I was there, eagerly learning all I could. I wanted to be used by God to help those who were sick or dying. It was a lifelong dream I yearned to attain.

CLOSER TO THE WHITE CAP

I continued to study and do as well as I could in every class, but I focused most intently on the courses required for the nursing program. I was also grateful for the wonderful math instructor I had. For the first time in my life, I really enjoyed math. He had us all call out, "I love math!" At the beginning of every class. By the time the semester was over, we really believed it! His encouraging method of teaching gave me the understanding I would need to easily calculate proper medication doses. Many nursing students struggled with that, and would drop out of the program because of it.

I was in my second year of studies, and had completed most of the prerequisites for the nursing program, when I got a letter from the Nursing Program Director. I screamed and ran around the house rejoicing, as I read that I had been accepted into the Nursing Program! I could not contain my excitement! There was a list of things I would need to do, the first was to meet for orientation to the program. Just after I received the letter, I was in my car, and looked over at the woman in the car next to me at a stop light. She had the white uniform of a nursing student, with the recognizable patch on her upper arm of our nursing program. *Soon, I will be wearing that!* I thought to myself, and tears of joy at the thought of it, rolled down my cheeks, and I laughed, praising God for His mercy and guidance in my life.

Orientation was exciting, but also a bit disheartening. There would be no white cap for me! The students had voted it down just the year before, and it would not be reinstated. I still managed to retain some of the image I had in my heart, because they gave us the choice of school uniforms; pants with a top and jacket, or a dress with a jacket. If you chose the dress, you would have to wear white stockings, with your white nursing shoes! I swooned at the thought! I was one of only two or three in the entire class of 90, to choose the dress! But it was a dear image I held to tightly, remembering the sweet nurse who I came to idolize as the perfect nurse. The nurse I longed to be.

THE CALL TO ARMS

We lost several hopeful nurses-to-be, when they found out during orientation the extent of time involved. It did not fit in with most work schedules. Good thing! This would not be a part-time endeavor. This was "Boot Camp" in every sense of that title. Our first clinical day, our uniforms were waiting, and we all eagerly put them on, with a sense of awe and excitement. I had brought the white stockings and the pretty, new, white, nursing shoes! They hardly made a sound as I walked! And like boot camp, something had to be done with our hair; thankfully we were not required to cut it. But those of us with long hair, learned quickly how to wear it up and out of the way. We were encouraged to finish dressing quickly, in order to prepare for our first clinical. We had a hard time concentrating on getting dressed, when there were two rooms full of hospital beds, and waiting "patients!" They had manikins with all the details of a real person awaiting our care. We were taught first how to change the bedding with the "patient" in the bed. (I have never forgotten the clever way they taught us to put on a pillow case!) Once the bed was made correctly, after being inspected, we learned basic care, like bathing and changing briefs. We would advance to things like oxygen administration, nasogastric tube insertion and removal, and Foley catheter insertion. Insertion was easy for most of us, but it was remembering all of the steps of the sterile procedure before and after that took practice. I made my own manikin at home to practice on. We learned many other basics those first few clinicals, before they announced that we would be learning how to start an IV, and we would be doing it on each other! We had to "jump in the water," so to speak, to learn. Most of us did quite well. Then we learned how to work the IV pumps, with all of the bells and whistles! I liked the machinery! It was a while before we were allowed on the hospital nursing floors. At first, we just followed our assigned nurse, observing and helping where needed. Soon, we were told we would have our own patients! We had to go to the assigned nursing floor beforehand, to choose a patient from the charts, that had difficulties similar to what we were studying in our lectures. I was so excited! I had an interest in caring for terminal patients, so that is what I looked for. I chose a middle-aged woman, with cancer that had spread (metastasized) to her brain. I was determined to give her the best possible care. That morning, when I introduced myself to her, she had been crying, and was agitated. I noticed that a relative was sitting near the TV, the volume was up on a news program, showing upsetting images and violence. He was not paying attention to it, because he was talking loudly on the phone. We had been taught, that patients with brain issues, needed a calm, quiet environment without much input. Too much noise and input would cause agitation and upset the patient. I backed out of the room, found my instructor and told her what I had observed, and she said, "Nurse, go back in there and advocate for your patient." Music to my ears! Just what I was hoping she would say. As I approached her room, a family member was in the doorway, tearful, and asked me about her condition. I answered her questions, and then I explained to her about decreasing the noise and stimulation to help calm her loved one down. She was more than eager to go in and turn off the TV and tell her relative to end his phone call and keep his voice down. When they knew how to help, they were more than eager to, and thankful that she calmed right down after that. Later, as I was helping my patient, she suddenly snapped at me, and became upset. I apologized and let her rest, knowing it was probably due to her brain cancer. A short time later when I went to check on her, she was tearful, so I approached her with compassion. She immediately reached out for my hand and squeezed it tightly as she said, "I'm so sorry! I don't know why I was mean to you. That's not like me!" I reassured her that I understood, and that it was not her, but the cancer that was causing those reactions. She was so relieved, thanking me and apologized again for how she treated me. I was so touched and grateful to be able to comfort her.

> Therefore comfort each other and edify one another. (1 Thessalonians 5:11)

MY CALLING REVEALED

The next day, my patient's doctor had ordered hospice services, and the hospice team had arrived to admit her to their hospice care. I listened carefully to everything that was discussed, and was so impressed with the loving approach of the hospice nurse and social worker, as they explained their services to my patient and her family. Her family was so relieved. Here, was my very first clinical patient, and she was going on hospice services. The Lord spoke to my heart, and I knew that was my calling as a nurse.

From that point on, I always chose the terminal patients as a student nurse. And every one of them taught me so much. I have always been able to tell when someone was hurting, and that was invaluable as a nurse. As nursing students, we worked under the nurse who had been assigned to the patients we chose. Despite the busy day shift, they patiently instructed us, and guided us as we performed care. Those with high caseloads, let us perform most of the routine care on our own. I had chosen a patient with terminal cancer. My nurse left his routine care to me, and when I noticed that he had not taken any pain medication, and had obvious signs of pain, I calmly said to him, "You're hurting, aren't you?" "Yes." He admitted under his breath. I asked him why he hadn't called the nurse for pain medication, and he said, "I know how busy she is, and I didn't want to bother her." I talked to him about the importance of keeping up with the pain, so it wouldn't take as much medication to keep it under control. If he put it off, it would take a higher dose to bring it back down. He was grateful for my explanation, and agreed to take some pain medication. The next day, his partner came to visit, who was positive and cheerful, saying how much he was looking forward to caring for him when he went home. After his partner left, I noticed my patient looked concerned and sad. I asked if there was something he was concerned about, and hesitantly he said, "I don't want my partner to have to take care of me. I don't want to be a burden to him." The Lord led me in my response, as I told him that giving care to someone you love is a gift. I shared about caring for my grandmother, and what a blessing it was for me. Then I told him that care giving is a way to show that you love someone, and that it would help his partner to be able to show his love and be of practical help in some way, even though he cannot take away your illness. It was like a light went on in his mind, and it made sense to him. He cheered up, and happily accepted his partner's involvement in his care, when he was discharged later that day. By showing the love of Christ, and by guiding him in His love, I trusted that he might answer the call of God before he died.

There were so many who touched my heart and helped me become a compassionate, caring nurse. Through their heartache and pain, I learned what was most important in life, and it was not a paycheck. It was answering the call of God, no matter where it took me.

Many questioned my calling in hospice. My nursing instructors felt I would be a good psychiatric nurse, and my family was concerned about me going into such a "depressing career." But my sights were clear, I knew where God was leading me.

Nursing School was hard. I won't sugar coat it. Of the ninety nursing students that started, only half went on to completion. There were several divorces, and many dropped out due the strain on their relationships, or jobs. I was so blessed to have the constant support of my husband, daughter and son, and also my good friend Gretchen. Gretchen was a retired RN, who had become good friends with me from our women's Bible study group. She counseled me like no one else could do, having walked in my shoes so many years before me. She stayed active by counseling patients before we met, and then she became my friend, and my counselor, as I often called her when things would catch up to me. She was not one to console, as much as exhort, with the word of God. She encouraged me to step up to the calling that God had given me, and she prayed for me. I almost quit several times, but Dennis and Gretchen would not allow it! Their encouragement and steadfast support helped me to finally become a Registered Nurse.

A JOYOUS BLESSING

In the weeks before I would be graduating, something much more important was happening in our lives; Lisa, our daughter, had given birth to our first grandchild! Words cannot describe the wonderful feeling of seeing your daughter, giving birth to her own daughter. I was awe struck by her strength and determination to birth her child, despite the baby being in the wrong position. She came into the world "sunny-side-up," not an easy birth by far! Being there, as a mother, new grandmother, and soon-to-be nurse, was such an amazing experience! My heart nearly burst from my chest for joy, and thankfulness, that my daughter and granddaughter had made it through such a difficult birth. It was such a long, hard labor for my daughter, but she persevered beyond any woman I had seen in delivery. I was hoping her birthing experience would have been easier, but seeing her nursing her daughter, holding her close a few short minutes later, assured me that the hard labor they both endured, had bonded them forever.

Only a few days later my momma called, and said that she would be coming to visit her great-granddaughter, and to be with us for my graduation. I was thrilled, but my head was spinning with planning and preparation, at the same time that I was cramming for finals! It was a very busy few weeks, but I am so grateful that my momma came. We all went to get a four-generation photo taken on Mother's Day. I'm looking at it now as I write this. Four strong, capable women, although the one in my mother's arms, was only two weeks old then, she is just as strong and capable now, as her mother, and her grandmothers. Strong women run in my family, my grandma, her mother, and her grandma, all pillars of strength, who stood on the Rock of Jesus Christ.

Our strength is not our own, but by the Lord's strength we persevere.

> "Not by might nor by power, but by My Spirit,"
> says the LORD of Hosts. (Zechariah 4:6)

NIGHTINGALE'S LAMP

Finally, the day came for our Nursing Final and Pinning Ceremony. All in the same day! I was focused on passing my final, and I did great! We were instructed to wear our nursing school uniforms one last time for a group photo after our final. I have that photo framed and hanging in our home now.

Then it was back home to dress for the Pinning Ceremony. Dennis, Momma, our daughter Lisa, her husband with our newborn granddaughter, and our son Jonathan, were at home to greet me. It was a beautiful, sunny afternoon when we all headed to the college theater where the Pinning Ceremony would take place. My good friends, Bev and her husband Paul, from our home Bible study, and Gretchen, my nursing mentor, met us at the ceremony. They had all been so faithful in praying me through to this point. I went up on stage with my fellow nursing graduates, where we each had seats facing the audience. We had been given our Nursing Pins earlier, and we had them ready to be pinned on by our instructors.

After the welcoming addresses by our nursing professors, the time came for our Pinning Ceremony. We were called, one at a time, to come forward and be pinned by one of our instructors. I was pinned by my last semester instructor, a sweet, encouraging nurse. I was thrilled to have her pin me, and her eyes sparkled with approval. Afterwards, it was time for the lighting of the candles. I was thrilled that they were using small replicas of the type of lamp that Florence Nightingale had carried, given to each of us, with a candle waiting to be lit. When we all were ready, one of our Nursing Professors lit her candle, and then lit the first of our candles, and we each passed the light until they were all lit. They had lowered the lights in the theater, and it was a sweet, solemn moment. It meant so much more than just nursing to me, it represented the light of Christ that as Christians, we should all be spreading to those in darkness. The world so needs the light of Jesus Christ. Jesus said, "I am the light of the world. He who follows me shall not walk in darkness, but have the light of life." (John 8:12)

Then it was time for us as a class, to recite our class pledge, and how eager I was! I was thrilled that our class voted on using, The Florence Nightingale Pledge, as our class pledge. It meant so much to me.

The Florence Nightingale Pledge

> I solemnly pledge myself before God and in the presence of this assembly to pass my life in purity and to practice my profession faithfully. I will abstain from whatever is deleterious and

mischievous and will not take or knowingly administer any harmful drug. I will do all in my power to maintain and elevate the standard of my profession, and will hold in confidence all personal matters committed to my keeping and all family affairs coming to my knowledge in the practice of my calling. With loyalty I will endeavor to aid the physician in his work, and devote myself to the welfare of those committed to my care.

(Florence Nightingale)

After our pledge, the Dean of Nursing gave the closing message, again from Florence Nightingale.

> Nursing is an art: and if it is to be made an art, it requires an exclusive devotion as hard as a preparation as any painter's or sculptor's work; for what is the having to do with dead canvas or dead marble, compared with having to do with the living body, the temple of God's Spirit? It is one of the Fine Arts: I had almost said, the finest of Fine Arts. (Florence Nightingale)

Florence Nightingale was not just a pioneer in nursing, she was a believer who tried to live her life according to her Lord, as revealed in the Bible, specifically in the book of John. When other women of her upper-class world in England, were primping and learning those things that would lead them to a marriage of wealth and privilege, she shunned those superficial pursuits as she sought to answer the call of God in her life. God had called her to His service, she openly documented that, but she was not sure what that service was. Her heart for the poor and destitute, the sick and dying, led her on the path of that service. She suffered much, had to fight bureaucracy, and the leaders of the English Army, in order to bring compassionate, effective care to the thousands of wounded and dying soldiers of the Crimean War. God in His mercy provided support in the very person of Queen Victoria, who did all she could to support, finance and promote Florence's work in providing appropriate care for the Queen's soldiers, who were so loved by her and Florence. Queen Victoria was her great admirer, and supported her in all her endeavors in the field of nursing and beyond.

How appropriate that she was called, "The Lady with the Lamp," as Florence answered the call of God by spreading the light of His loving care to all she could. I wanted to be that light of Christ too.

Two other quotes of Florence Nightingale fit the sending out of our nursing class to serve as they had been taught.

> How very little can be done under the spirit of fear. (Florence Nightingale)

We are to go forward fearlessly in our calling, whatever that calling of God is for us. We are reminded in 2 Timothy 1:7 "For God has not given us a spirit of fear, but of power and of love and of a sound mind."

The second quote from Florence:

> Go your way straight to God's work, in simplicity
> and singleness of heart. (Florence Nightingale)

Indeed! All of us have a call from God to serve Him, in whatever capacity that might be. He has given us His Holy Spirit to lead us, strengthen us and inspire us in our individual callings. Not one of us can do this on our own, it is by the power and the very presence of Christ in our lives that we can answer the call of God. As it says in Acts 17:18, "For in Him we live and move and have our being,"

I walked out of the theater into the loving embrace of my family and friends, and was grateful that they were all able to meet the professors who had such an amazing impact on my life. I treasure the photos that captured those moments with our family and friends, and especially the one of my momma and Gretchen with my favorite Professor. It was a night I will always remember and treasure in my heart.

THANKFULLY HIRED

I woke up the next morning feeling as if I were in limbo. School was over, and I didn't have a job. Many of my classmates had already been offered positions and were working. I had hoped to be hired at the hospital where I had my preceptorship, but I had not heard back about my application. Then the phone rang, and it was another hospital offering me a position. It had good hours, but it was not where I was hoping to work. I was unsure and said I would get back to them. I prayed, asking God for direction, not wanting to close a door of opportunity, if it was the only offer I would receive. Later in the evening, the phone rang again, only this time it was the Director of Nursing, at the hospital I hoped would call! The same hospital our son was first taken to for his head trauma. She offered me a position in the department I was hoping for, where I had been a preceptor. What a weight was lifted from my shoulders! The hours weren't so great, but it didn't matter to me, so of course, I accepted her offer.

When I went in to meet the Director of Nursing, she asked

me what my goals were. I told her the truth. I was hoping to gain the experience I would need to move on to a career in hospice nursing. I also told her, I was dedicated to being the best nurse possible and a valuable team member in their unit. She appreciated my candor, and welcomed me to the unit. I rejoiced as I left the hospital, praising God in my car, for His mercy and direction in my life, opening the path before me.

The hospital where I was hired, was dedicated to supporting and educating their new graduate nurses. We all met together, at our first hospital orientation. There were almost a dozen new nurses! I was thrilled to see several other graduates from my class. Orientation was enlightening and exciting, as they taught us their core values, and protocols. It also involved having us shadow nurses in different units, so we could experience areas other than the ones we were hired for. I had the opportunity to follow a nurse in the maternity unit, and was able to provide a comforting presence for a woman who had just lost her newborn in childbirth the night before. How hard it must have been for her, but she seemed comforted by my supportive presence. Sometimes just being there, is a comfort to those who are grieving. Words cannot help at times like that. That experience helped to confirm my calling in hospice. It was where God was leading me.

After several orientation meetings, they had us all vote for those of us, who best represented the five core values. I was humbled, but thrilled when my fellow nurses chose me for the core value of "Service." That was all I wanted to do, to serve the Lord in whatever way I could.

As we rotated to different units, I became quite thankful

for being hired in the unit I had chosen. I would be in a cardiac unit, where patients would come for heart surgery and recovery, and with any heart condition, no matter what their primary diagnosis was. All of the other units just didn't work for me in one way or another. My instructors thought I would like Oncology; but during my rotation there, I was sickened at the thought of injecting toxic therapies into cancer patients, hoping for a healing. I knew that sometimes, it worked; but I did not feel led to be the one administering such drugs.

I was eager to start my regular shift in my unit. It would be difficult working twelve-hour shifts at night! We had three work nights a week, and they usually worked us two nights in a row, off one or two, and then another work night, to help us adjust during the days we were off. It was strange being awake in the daytime; I felt like I was in a dream state, and I didn't function so well. But I was fine at work, learning more and more with every shift. I was grateful that the doctors often admitted patients with varying diagnoses to our unit, with a lower patient to nurse ratio. This allowed me to care for patients with a wide assortment of ailments, teaching me more than if I was in a different unit. I also noticed how most of the nurses in my unit did not want patients who were terminal. It was a cultural thing for some, and for the others, it was understandable, because most nurses want to heal people, not see them die. I had a different calling, and told the charge nurses that I would be happy to take the terminal patients. They were happy to let me, because none of them wanted to lose a patient in their care; however, I felt it was an honor. I knew it was important to help bring comfort and quality to their last hours.

I loved working nights! Despite the difficult adjustment to daytime, nights were the best time for interacting with patients. There were no visits from concerned families, no doctor visits, no meals, none of the regular busy hospital activities. In the solitude of the nights, patients often would open up to me. They would tell me how they really felt, needing a compassionate, understanding listener. The terminal patients I cared for, were the most affected by the busy, hustle of the day shift. Visiting family members meant well, but often were not willing to accept a terminal diagnosis. Many terminal patients accept their diagnosis long before their loved ones do. They actually looked forward to the nights, when they didn't have to be explaining things to worried loved ones. I cared for many terminal patients, having the honor of caring for nine patients as they died, in the two years I worked there. Much more than the other nurse's entire careers. I was grateful that the charge nurses entrusted me with the care of those terminal patients. Most of the ones I cared for were comfortable as they passed, but a few were in pain up to the end, due to the doctor's refusal to increase their pain medication. Doctors are trained to heal people; they don't ever want to lose a patient. On rare occasions, a few tried to prolong the patient's life, by withholding appropriate, pain medication. That is not only unwise, but cruel to the patient and family members, who suffer along with them as their loved one is racked with pain and unable to interact with them. As nurses, we can request a change in the medication orders, but it is up to the physician to make that change. The hardest assignment I ever had there, was a patient who had a very painful illness that was taking his life. Unfortunately, his doctor was a friend, and the doctor wanted to do all he could to delay his death. In that effort, he ordered no pain medication, except for Tylenol PRN (as needed); and as his friend writhed in pain, the doctor ordered restraints, so he would not hurt himself as he thrashed on his bed. I did all in my power to convince the doctor, my charge nurse tried too, but he was resolute in his orders. I spent most of my shift at this dying man's bedside, giving the best comfort I could with what I was allowed to use, taking every opportunity to whisper the love of Jesus Christ in his ear. His death was a sweet release, as all the agony of his pain melted away in peace. There was no sign of pain on his face, just sweet serenity. I prayed that he was in the arms of Jesus, and trusted God for that. I accompanied him down to the hospital morgue, feeling so protective of this man who had suffered so much. I *needed* to move on to hospice! I could not tolerate the idea of seeing another person passing in agony.

I am so thankful as I write this, that caring for terminal patients has greatly improved! Most physicians now recognize the benefits of hospice, and many hospitals have palliative care programs, to help ease the terminal patient's pain and provide support and encouragement for their families. This also provides an easier transition for the patient, leading naturally to hospice care as they decline. What a blessing that hospice care has now become a team effort with the patient's physicians and hospital staff.

I had been working there almost two years, before the Lord impressed upon me the need to move on. My good friend and a fellow nursing graduate, was already working as a hospice nurse for another hospice, and he was a great inspiration for me. My supervisor was sad to see me go, but very encouraging; she knew that was where God was leading me. There were a few hospices in town, but I found the perfect fit at another hospital's hospice service. The peace of God washed over me as I went in for the interview, and I knew that God had led me there.

> Trust in the LORD with all your heart,
> And lean not on your own understanding;
> In all your ways acknowledge Him,
> And He shall direct your paths. (Proverbs 3:5–6)

WELCOMED TO HOSPICE

I felt so blessed to have been hired by such a wonderful hospice. My supervisor was so sweet and encouraging. I felt so invigorated working a day shift! I had a lot to learn; hospice nursing has its own protocols, and medications for comfort. I spent the first weeks, studying and making visits with various hospice workers. My first visit with a hospice nurse, was to check on a patient who was imminent (close to passing). I watched closely as the nurse encouraged the patient and family members. She assessed him for signs of discomfort, giving instructions to the family before we left, and reminded them to call with any changes. When we walked to her car, she saw I was smiling, and asked me why. I told her that I could not help myself, I realized I was where God wanted me to be, I belonged in hospice. In those first few weeks, I went out to visits with other nurses, a health aide, a social worker, and a pastoral counselor, to observe their roles in hospice services. I was really impressed with all of their roles, but so thankful for the social workers! They took care of all of the things I had been concerned about trying to do. Answering all of the family's questions about insurance, Medicare and the things I knew little about; as well as providing emotional support. My role as a hospice case managing nurse included: providing the physical care, keeping the patient comfortable, teaching and encouraging the family members, providing needed supplies, ordering equipment as needed in the course of decline, managing the medications, coordinating the other hospice services, and communicating with the physician, regarding patient changes or new orders. Most of the physicians turned over the care of their patients to our Medical Director, which made communication much easier. Hospice had meetings once a week, where the whole team would meet with our Medical Director and discuss the care and condition of each of our patients. It was really helpful and insightful, as we all worked together to assure we had a good plan of care for each patient and their family members. Hospice was about the care of the whole family. It is a hard thing to accept hospice services. For many it feels like they are "giving up." Hospice encourages and teaches them that the last days of their loved one's life can be fulfilling and meaningful.

It does take a team to properly care for hospice patients and their families, and I would come to really appreciate their help in caring for each of my patients. It was a new experience for me to make nursing visits alone, not having another nurse on hand to help move a patient or while performing a needed procedure. But we were always able to call for help if needed. I quickly learned to do all that had to be done on my own when needed. We did arrange our visits with other team members routinely, always at the first home visit after admission to our services. But also, to visit with our social worker or home health aide, presenting as a team. The home health aides, were loving pillars of support for the patients. With hands on care, they bathed them, applied lotions, dressed them, washed and brushed their hair, and shaved the men, all while encouraging them with their kindness and loving care. They were hard working and so valuable as teammates, letting us know about any subtle changes in our patients. With such close, loving care, our patients often bonded quickly with our caregivers.

The social workers usually carried heavier caseloads than the nurses, so matching schedules took a bit of work. Family members appreciated those joint visits, that gave the nurse the opportunity to take care of the patient's needs, while the social worker supported the caregiving family member. Hospice also provided volunteers to visit patients while the caregiver could go to the store or run an errand. Another favorite type of volunteer, were the hospice animal visits. Most hospices have volunteers available with therapy animals (mostly dogs), trained for patient visits. We also had music therapy volunteers who would bring their instrument and play for those who wanted it. Those types of special visits bring so much comfort and joy to the patients and their family members. Family caregivers can feel alone in caring for their loved one, but knowing that there was always someone who could come and support them, made the journey easier for them. I learned so much from each of the members of the hospice team, and I felt blessed to be a part of such a caring profession.

MY OWN CASELOAD

My supervisor assigned just six patients to me, the first week that I was making visits as a hospice RN case manager. Hospice provided me with all of the supplies my patients might need, along with a large nursing bag, filled with every possible item I might need in the field for patient care. They even gave me my own business cards! I was thrilled! My supervisor would quickly be adding to my case load, as I showed my capability to handle it. One of the things I enjoyed about my job, was the freedom I had in arranging my visits. It was up to me to assess the needs of each patient, and how often they should be seen. The typical visit schedule is for two to four visits a week for each patient, Monday through Friday, eight am to five pm. Some were stable at admission, and only needed a weekly visit, while others were actively declining, with rapidly changing conditions, that required frequent visits. My visits were also dependent on the patient and family members. Some only wanted one visit a week at first, even though more frequent visits were indicated.

They quickly realized how needful those visits were, and would allow me to come more often. We would have to earn the trust of our patients and family members, with every contact. They needed to feel secure with everything we did, and by respecting their wishes, their trust came quickly. I loved the challenge of providing the best care possible, while balancing out the visits during each week. We also had to chart each visit on our laptop computers, so that it was readily available to the team. Our team included night nurses who covered after-hours and weekends. We communicated with the team using the pagers and mobile phones provided, mostly text messages. It was a whole new world of nursing for me!

As much as I appreciated all of the team members and all of the support, the focus for me was the people I came to know as I was welcomed in to share those precious last days with them and their families. To say that they were grateful for our care, would be an understatement. My heart trembled for them, as I perceived the anguish and helplessness in their faces, as they opened their door to us for that first visit. Our arrival was a breath of hope for them. So many were thinking that they would not be able to give the care that was needed for their loved one. Most did not know how they could do it. Our first visit, which included the social worker, was to lift the burden of concern, reassuring them that they would not be alone on this journey, and supplying everything they needed to go forward.

I loved seeing the expressions of relief, when they realized we could have a home health aide come to help with bathing, or that I would be able to provide the wound care or help manage the medications. Many of the family members had been bathing and caring for their loved one for a while, and the relief of having those harder tasks lifted from their shoulders was a blessing for them. I had felt that myself, when we first had home health aides come to help with my grandma. I was hesitant at first, wondering if they would be as loving and kind as I would be, but seeing my happy grandma was all the proof I needed! I always encouraged the family members, the same way my grandma's nurse encouraged me, saying, "This will give you the opportunity to be more of a spouse/daughter/son, than a caregiver." It was also a great relief to know they could call me or hospice at any time with questions, concerns or changes in their loved one. They seemed surprised when I answered promptly. Sometimes they just needed to know they were not alone, and I always did my best to arrive swiftly for any concern.

One of my first patients was a strong, healthy man, barely sixty years old, who had a stomach ache, and went to his doctor. Unfortunately, he received a grim diagnosis, stage four cancer. He was given just a few weeks to live. When I arrived for the first visit, hospice had already provided a hospital bed, and he was laying in pain in that bed, set up in their dining room. I asked his worried wife if they had received the hospice emergency kit, and thankfully it had just arrived. I gave him an appropriate dose of pain medication, before assessing him. He appeared to be rapidly declining. His wife told me that he had only seen the doctor the week before, and that he was up and showered himself yesterday, and even ate a hardy steak dinner. Then she asked me how long I thought it would be. My mind raced! What could I tell her? His vital signs and increasing pain, all pointed to a rapid passing. But what she told me about the last twenty-four hours, gave me pause. I learned from this experience, not to give an estimate of time. Only God knows, and with later patient's families, I would usually say that the time was between God and the patient. Experience gave me more insight into when that might be, but even then, it is in God's hands.

So I told her, "Maybe a week? It's hard to say." Those words to this loving, hopeful wife, would break my heart, as he died the very next day. I felt I had taken away that week she thought she had! I was so devastated. I learned about the Lord's sovereignty with that strong, healthy-looking man. I learned that God is the only One who knows the day and the moment of our passing.

I also came to learn with every experience I had, that only the Lord, could give me the peace I needed, to be His hand extended. It was the peace of Christ, and His unshakeable presence, that was able to bring calm into some of the most horrific circumstances. A hospice nurse, must present a calm professionalism. There is no place for panic or excitability. Only Christ can impart that kind of peace, and He was there with me, every step of the way. I saw how His amazing grace, could bring peace, even in the toughest situations.

I was called to the home of a patient who was in severe distress. His nurse was at a visit quite far away, and I was nearby, so my supervisor sent me, telling me what was happening. I prayed for the Lord to help me, and arrived quickly, to find the patient close to passing, no signs of pain, but with disturbing symptoms that frightened the family. It was the calming peace of Christ that allowed me to be able to calm the family, because they felt His peace through me, as I cared for their loved one. They were able to spend precious time with him, just before he passed, and were calm and thankful for his gentle passing. It was the Holy Spirit's presence, that covered them in peace. Only the Lord can bring such peace in situations like those.

> "With men this is impossible, but with God all things are possible." (Jesus, Matthew 19:26)

When I left, I only felt thankfulness to the Lord, for being able to meet the needs of that patient and family, and the grimness of it was washed away with his peaceful passing and a family that had been comforted. I knew that it was not by my strength, but by God's mercy, that I was able to remain calm. God was with me through every visit, leading me and shining through me, so others might see Him. And they often did.

THEY DID NOT SEE ME

We made visits to see our patients wherever they might be living. Sometimes in the hospital at admission, mostly in their home or apartment, and also in long term care facilities, or group homes. We gave the same support and care, working with the staff to promote the comfort and care of our patients. It was at a group home, where I first came to realize, that they did not always see "me" when I was there.

I had a sweet elderly lady at a group home, whose daughter made frequent visits, and I often met with her during my visits. Her mother was declining, and not responsive during my visit, when she told me that her mother said, she had seen an angel. The caregiver came in and said that she also had told her the same thing, and during those times, I had just visited her. I was shocked! But then I realized, whenever I visited her, I would whisper how the Lord Jesus loved her in her ear. Her sight was poor, so she must have thought I was an angel, or maybe she saw past me, into the spiritual realm. I certainly don't look like an angel! But the Lord often uses us to reach out and call His lambs home to Him. I always let my patients know that Jesus loved them. We were not allowed to "proselytize," at work, but the Lord always arranged times alone, to whisper the love of Jesus to these precious souls. I always knew that the Lord had reached out to them before I came along, and I trusted Him to lead them to salvation. I am sure that most of those I cared for, passed into eternity with the Lord. Often by the things they told me before they died. Like, "I saw Jesus standing at the foot of my bed!" Or that they had seen their loved ones who were in heaven. Many of them, I saw lifting their hands up into the air, as if reaching out for the Lord, in the moments before they passed. Throughout those years as a hospice nurse, I came to realize that our loving Father never lets anyone leave without revealing Himself to them in some way.

Having the opportunity, to be in the presence of those who were passing, made me a witness, a blessed spectator to the magnificent love and calling of the Lord, as He reached out to so many. I could only stand amazed, and pray in thanksgiving to the One who loves us so!

> I drew them with gentle cords, With bands of love, And I was to them as those who take the yoke from their neck. (Hosea 11:4)

"I'M AN AGNOSTIC"

Not all of my patients were open to the idea of an afterlife. As a Christian, I allowed the Lord in His wisdom, to direct my interaction with each individual. For some, I might be the only example of Christ they would see.

This is the story of an amazing man, that I had the privilege to care for. He was a man of means, living in a beautiful apartment in the upper floor of an exclusive, assisted living facility. He had an amazing collection of souvenirs from around the world on display, having traveled often in his life. He had wonderful manners, and a slight accent from his original home overseas. He introduced himself as a scientist, and then he said, "I'm an agnostic." (An agnostic is "someone who does not know, or believes that it is impossible to know, if a god exists." From the Cambridge English Dictionary) I was surprised by his statement, as we do not tell patients what our personal beliefs are, so he did not know that I was a Christian. I felt he wanted to make sure that I knew where he stood. I told him, "That's fine." And I thought he may be trying to illicit a response from me, to tell him where I stood. But I did not take the bait. After I had answered his questions about hospice, and completed an assessment with vital signs, he asked if he could show me around the facility. He had a balcony overlooking a lush, tropical garden below on the first floor, in the center of the oval shaped building, that was open to the sky, and all the apartments had a view of the garden. He took me down to the first floor, and outside to walk through the gardens, with gazebos and benches along the way to rest. He was still quite capable of walking, and eager to show me all of the amenities, such as the exercise room, and other activity rooms, within the first floor, facing the garden. We came to the far end of the garden, where a large covered bridge went over the babbling brook that ran around the perimeter of the garden. As we crossed, there was a joyous celebration of some sort there, and people were dressed up for the occasion, champagne glasses in hand. I was impressed by all that this luxury building had to offer; but my scientist patient, seemed less impressed, despite this tour he had initiated. Money can buy many things, but it cannot satisfy the longing heart, that empty hole in our souls, that only God can fill. He became silent, and then said good-bye, assuring me that he would be able to make it back to his apartment on his own.

 I loved visiting him. He was so engaging and knowledgeable about so many things. He wanted me to tell him exactly how he was doing with each visit, and I explained to him why there was a change in his vital signs, appetite, and pain level. Most people want to know what is happening to their bodies as they decline, some do not. It took discernment to perceive what each patient really wanted to know. He was accepting his decline as an inevitable reality, with mature graciousness. I wondered if he was thinking about what would happen after his death. He was a logical scientist, but logic can only resolve material things, not the things of the heart and spirit.

He started declining, and the time came when he could no longer get out of bed, and I went in to visit him, making sure he was comfortable and his symptoms were well managed. After my exam was complete, he looked away, as if working up the courage, and then turned his eyes to me and said, "Denise, I think I must be losing my mind." As calmly as if he had asked for a drink of water. I responded, just as calmly, "What makes you think that?" And he said, "I'm seeing," and he paused before saying, "apparitions." "Really?" I replied. "What did they look like?" He paused again, thinking before answering, "I think they must be angels." Then he described seeing them, floating around his bed, beautiful and bright like the sun, as if they were watching over him. He said he felt such peace when they were there. It must have been quite difficult for him to be able to tell me this, knowing how his scientific mind must have been struggling with the reality of what he was experiencing. I gently responded, "You know, there is more to us than just our flesh." He thought about what I said for a moment, and then he said, "I think you must be right." Then I told him that he should think about what he was seeing. And that there was a spiritual dimension beyond what we can usually see, and that he was blessed to be glimpsing a part of it. I so wanted to tell him all about Jesus! But instead, I prayed fervently for him when I left, and kept him in my prayers, praying that the Lord would draw this lamb into his bosom. Then, a few days later, I got the call that he had passed away, and went to attend his death. He was lying in his bed, with the most serene, relaxed expression on his face, almost smiling. I prayed that he was with the Lord Jesus, and after they had taken him away, my social worker arrived, and told me details given to her from the volunteer who had been visiting him and playing chess with him. I had only met him briefly, a tall, handsome young man, but did not know much about him. Then my social worker told me that he was a Christian, and that our patient and him had become quite close, and when he felt himself fading, he called for this young man to come, and he was there as he passed. Oh, praise the Lord for His loving mercy! The Lord sent another believer to bridge the gap that I had left! I fully trust that my sweet scientist, is making wonderous discoveries in heaven with the Lord.

The Lord loves us so! He longs for us all to come to Him for salvation! He would have no one lost, but still He allows us the choice to choose Him over death eternal. How heartbroken the Lord must be, when someone chooses death over eternal life with Him, our loving Savior.

I had learned years before, about the broken heart of God, when those who choose to reject Him, pass into darkness, forever, without Him.

THE HEART OF OUR FATHER

Many years ago, my sweet grandma left my grandpa when things were hard between them. She had been wooed away by a sinful man. She had no idea that he was a sweet-talker, an alcoholic, and had a vile reputation. No one in the family was happy about her choice, especially because he kept putting off marrying her. No one wanted to visit her while he was there, and he always was. Momma would take me with her, when I was young, and she would go to pick up Grandma for a visit. He would always try to draw us in to stay, his eyes set on me. But Momma knew better! She always made a quick exit with me and Grandma. None of the other family members would let their children near him, so Grandma was broken-hearted over the separation from her children. Even years later, when he finally married her, it did not repair the rift between him and the family.

Through the years, we had Grandma over often, relishing our time with her. She was such a delightful, fun, and yet gracious lady. Momma had many family gatherings, for Easter, Thanksgiving, and on Grandma's birthdays. That way, the rest of the family was able to visit with her too.

Then, after I was married, my momma noticed that Grandma had started drinking along with him, and her heath took a nose-dive. Momma would not have it! She took Grandma away from him, bringing her to live with them, nursing her back to health, and clearing the alcohol from her system. During that time, Momma would take Grandma to his house, once a week, to pick up her mail. Then one time, Grandma came back to the car, without the mail, and said, "He's gone." Momma thought she meant he wasn't there, but then Grandma told her she thought he might be dead. Momma went in and found him, in his chair, obviously dead for some time. As hard as it was for Momma to see, it must have been even harder for poor Grandma! Momma came out swiftly, and called the authorities.

As the news reached me, the family was rejoicing that he was dead. There was no grieving, no sadness, except for my grandma, who didn't really know what to feel, except that she had lost her husband, and the family was rejoicing. It broke my heart! A man had died, and there was no sorrow or loss shown in my family. I couldn't get over it. Even though I knew he was an evil man, and had almost dragged Grandma down with him, I was heartbroken. I prayed to God, asking Him why it hurt me so much; and then, I asked Him to show me what He felt, at the loss of this soul. I was weeping as I prayed, pouring out my heart to Him, when suddenly, He gave me just a moments glimpse into His heart. It is impossible to explain the depth of sorrow the Lord revealed to me. Even though it was just a brief moment's look into His heart, it overwhelmed my own heart with such a profound grief, as He revealed the darkness that man had entered, and the sorrow God felt at his death. I wept that whole day, unable to fathom the depth of love our loving Father has for each one of us! Oh, how He loves us! He truly is *not* willing that *any* should perish!

> The Lord is not slack concerning His promise, as some count slackness, but is longsuffering towards us, not willing that any should perish but that all should come to repentance. (2 Peter 3:9)

SLIPPING AWAY

As I gained more experience as a hospice nurse, I discovered that most patients die at night, slipping away, often unnoticed until morning. I always felt a loss when that happened, not being the one to attend the death and comfort the family that I had been visiting. I was grateful for our night nurses, who were well seasoned and excellent at coming along aside the families at those times. But closure was difficult. As I had been working there awhile, they started giving me a monthly rotation, where I was on call one or two nights. This was shared by the rest of the nurses, in order to give the night nurses vacations or sick days. It was hard to go to sleep those nights, wondering if the phone would ring. When it did, I dressed swiftly and went out to take care of whatever the emergency was. Often it was the passing of a patient. Then it was my turn to comfort a grieving family and care for their loved one, that I had never met. The tenderness of those who grieve, endeared them to me. I felt as if I had always known them. They were so receptive to my presence and care.

I found that it brought great comfort to the family, to see their loved one at peace, with no signs of pain or suffering. This is one of the benefits of hospice services in a person's own home. When a hospice nurse attends a death, we first confirm the passing and the time, then we wash and dress the patient according to the family's wishes. Sometimes, if the family seemed willing, I would offer to let them wash their loved one's face, or any other care they might want to provide. Sometimes the family had already washed and dressed them, before we would arrive.

I will never forget one family, that had prepared their mother before I arrived. It was a surprise to me and my social worker, who were arriving for our first visit, and our patient passed away before we got there. We noticed there were many family members there, and wondered about it, until the daughter told us as we entered, that their mother had passed away a short time before we arrived. They had lovingly cleaned her and dressed her in her favorite peignoir set. They told us happily, that it was an agreement between her and their late father, that they would be buried in outfits that they each would recognize, when they were reunited in heaven. They had dressed their father in his favorite leisure suit, and they chose the last peignoir set that he had bought her as a gift for Christmas before he passed. They said he bought her a new peignoir set every Christmas during their marriage. Her children beamed, as they told us this, and were thrilled to think of them seeing each other, and finally being reunited in heaven. What a sweet way to honor them.

Most family members just wanted to hold their hand, and spend time with them once they were clean and cared for. I often spoke gently to the one who passed, telling them what I was doing as I washed them and dressed them. It was a respectful thing to do. Honoring the vessel that God had made, and once held the soul of a living person. The families always took comfort in the way we cared for their loved ones. That's how I would want someone to care for my loved one. In those visits, I knew that the loved one was no longer there. That is one of the reasons I encouraged family members to hold their hand, or stroke their face. Touch alone reveals that they are not there. It is a testimony that our bodies are only the vessels of the life within, and when that life has left, only the empty vessel remains behind. Knowing that their loved one is no longer bound to the body of their suffering, gives a sense of relief for the grieving family. It gives them a sense of closure, helping with the process of grieving. I always remained with the family until the funeral home would arrive and take their loved one into their care. It is hard to have them leave, and providing support is so important.

Although many of my own patients passed at night, I often had the privilege of being at their bedside as they began to pass, and I would stay with them throughout that time. When their breath begins to fade, first rapid, and then shallow, with long gaps in between breaths, I would know it was close. Encouraging loved ones to say those things they wanted to say, reminding them that science had proven, that the last thing to go is hearing, despite their lack of response. I even had a patient who was quite deaf, and when she was close to passing, she called out to her daughter, saying, "What is all of that noise outside?" Someone was mowing their lawn, and she would have never heard that normally. God is so wonderful, the way He orchestrates the events leading to the death of our bodies. He often allows those with dementia, to have brief "windows" of clarity, where they can interact with their family members, responding verbally, when they had been non-verbal for quite some time. I saw that so often! Sometimes the family would think that they were improving, and might live. We always encouraged them to take advantage of those fleeting periods of clarity, and tell their loved one what they have been longing to say. The Lord is so merciful!

A social worker told me about a lady who had dementia, and as she declined, she could no longer walk. Just before she passed away, she had that brief time of clarity, and was able to get up and dance with her husband, to their favorite song, just before she died. What a blessing it must have been, for her, her grieving husband, and her family.

IN HIS TIME

Sometimes, people do not pass when we expect them to. But there always seemed to be a reason behind it. I will never forget the passing of a woman, in her sixties, with her two daughters caring for her. Despite her fading vital signs, she was not passing. Her daughters were exhausted, keeping constant vigil. They were expressing their concern about what may be keeping their mother from letting go. So the social worker asked if there was something left undone, or someone she hadn't said good-bye to. Both sisters looked at each other, and then told us that they had another sister in another state, but she had a disagreement with their mother, and they had not spoken to each other for years. The social worker asked if they would be willing to call their sister and let her know that their mother was passing, and they both agreed. They got her on the phone, and after telling her what was happening, they put the phone up to their mother's ear. She had not been responsive, but at the voice of her estranged daughter, she woke up and she was able to say, "I love you," to her daughter. There were tears and thankfulness for the daughters and their mother. She died a short time after that phone call, peacefully, with two daughters at her side, and their estranged sister comforted, knowing her mother loved her.

That type of thing happened more often than you could imagine. I had a patient who was admitted to hospice services after all medical intervention had failed. We often get patients when they are very close to passing. Some pass before we make that first visit. I was quick to make the first visit, understanding that he was well on his way. He was an older man, married many years to a wonderful woman. She was beside herself with worry, because he was fading fast, and their son, who was across the states, would not arrive to see him until late Friday. It was a Tuesday when I visited. He had every sign that he should not last a day, let alone three days. He had long pauses between breaths, and was not responsive. His wife asked me if he would last until their son arrived. Even though it appeared that he could pass at any time, and yet knowing that people often surprise us, I told her the truth; that it was possible, but to be prepared that he might not make it until his son arrives. I also told her I would be praying for them. She told me she was telling him often, that their son was arriving Friday, and to hold on, despite his lack of responsiveness. I checked on him each day, with no change. Friday came, and he was still with us, and still not responsive. My shift ended, and I didn't hear what had happened until the Monday report saying that he had passed. I called that precious wife, and she told me, that her husband waited until his son arrived, woke up and was able to speak with his son for an hour before he drifted off to sleep, and passed a short time later. Oh, the loving mercy of the Lord!

Sometimes, people slip away at times we don't expect. This can cause heartache for a loved one who wants to be there for their passing, and they miss it!

NO GOOD-BYE

I loved this precious, elderly couple! They were both in their nineties, and he was placed on hospice services. They had a wonderful caregiver, who cooked and cleaned for them. She was a cheerful, loving caregiver. The couple were both lively characters! The wife was a tiny woman with a hot temper, who would yell at her husband and they would banter back and forth, quite common for them. But despite their feistiness, their love for each other filled the air in their little apartment. I was visiting more frequently as he started to decline, and his little wife sat in a chair right next to the bed to be as close as possible to him. She watched me like a hawk when I would come to examine him, making sure I was not hurting him. Then I got a call from the frantic caregiver, "Help me, help me! She's hitting me! Her husband has died, and she's blaming me!" I quickly went to their home, and the caregiver rushed to let me in, as his broken-hearted wife retreated to the bedroom to sit next to the body of her beloved. Then the caregiver told me, that while the wife was sitting by her husband's bedside, the caregiver answered a phone call, and it was a family member wanting to talk to the wife. So the caregiver told her she had a call, and the wife left his side to answer the call. When she returned, he had passed away. She was furious and blamed the caregiver for missing his passing. When I entered the room, she was sitting in the chair next to him, solemn, with her head down. I told her how sorry I was for her loss, and she wept as she said she had wanted to be with him when he died, and to say good-bye. I said, "I know. You really loved him, didn't you?" "Yes," she said, quietly. I responded, "He really loved you too." "Yes, he did," she acknowledged. Then I said, "He loved you so much, he wanted to spare you seeing him die, and so he waited for you to leave, before he let go, and passed." "Really?" She said eagerly. "Yes," I said, "I've seen this happen before." Suddenly her anger melted away at the thought of him waiting for her to leave, so he could spare her. The spark of love for her husband was shining in her eyes, as she watched me carefully, making sure I did not disturb him. She did allow me to listen for a heartbeat, touching him only with the stethoscope. She only got up when their clergy arrived, and she hugged their caregiver, telling her she was sorry, and telling her that he loved her too much to let her see him die. They both cried together.

The older generation, often waits for family to leave the room, before they pass. I had a gentleman with dementia in a care facility, who was taking a long time to pass. His family members, six or seven people were at his bedside, counting the seconds, almost a minute between his breaths, and wondering why he had not passed. I told them that often folks wait until family members leave before they pass. So they all went into the hallway and waited, as I stood in the doorway. It was only a few minutes before he passed, and the family felt as if they had given him a gift, by letting him pass in peace.

I trust that the Lord is reaching out to those who linger. From those who were able to tell me what they were experiencing, I know that the Lord reaches out to folks, in a way unique to each one. Just like the verse I quoted earlier, in Hosea 11:4, the Lord draws them with tender cords; He knows their hearts, and will draw all those to Him, "But only those who are written in the Lamb's Book of Life." (Revelation 21:27)

Some do not accept His salvation, until the very last moment. Like the thief on the cross with Jesus, who asked for His mercy, and Jesus assured him, that he would be there with Him that day, in paradise. (Luke 23:43) Jesus only requires us to believe in Him, no works are required.

> For by grace you have been saved through faith, and that not of yourselves; it is the gift of God, not of works, lest anyone should boast. (Ephesians 2:8–9)

We do not know what may be happening in that spiritual place, where our loved ones, so close to death, have glimpses of the spiritual realm. We cannot see what they may be seeing, we can only trust in the loving mercy of our Lord. Knowing what a loving Savior Jesus is, I trust Him with my loved ones.

> But as many as received Him, to them He gave the right to become children of God, to those who believe in His name. (John 1:12)

ON HOLY GROUND

Being there, as these precious souls passed from the earthly realm, and on to the spiritual realm, was holy ground for me. I never lost that sense of awe, in those precious moments. After my first few years as a hospice nurse, I wrote a poem about that time of spiritual transition, in 2004. I called it, "Heaven's Gate."

> What a privilege to dwell here;
> a place warm with heart and tears.
> A place where all that is superficial
> falls away in the face of pure humanity.
> A place where hope is tenderly courted
> and sweet memories become a cool enveloping
> pool of mercy.
> How soft and fragile the delicate skin

that awaits its blooming hour.
An hour clothed in mystery;
a time both feared and yearned for.
Where the chains of this world fall away,
and we burst forth in freedom.
I close my eyes in reverence
here in this place,
Dwelling near Heaven's Gate.

A SLOWER PACE

Suddenly, we found ourselves moving out of state to be near our daughter and grandchild when they needed to move. We did not think I would have to continue nursing, and I was looking forward to retiring and having the time to spend with our grandchild. It was such a beautiful, comforting place to live. It reminded me of my childhood home, with old trees lining the streets, branches shading the homes, with many front porches, and friendly neighbors. I discovered spring, for the first time in my life! I was raised in the sun belt, where flowers bloomed year-round. I had no idea that the seemingly bare dirt, could suddenly bloom! It was my first March in our home, when I was walking around the yard, as the snow was melting back, that I saw something bright purple. It was a Crocus! I was thrilled! I started recording every new bloom in a garden notebook, writing down the dates of every new flower rising up out of the ground. Crocus were first, then Hyacinth, Tulips, Lily of the Valley and so many more! But none of them gave me as much joy, as seeing small spots of purple and lavender all over our lawn, realizing that my very favorite flower and scent, Violets, were growing like scattered gems across our property! I felt as if it were a blessing from God. I knew we were where He wanted us to be. I was shocked to learn that locals often considered them weeds! Such a heavenly, powdery scent, would waft in the air as I walked through the yard.

At first, I did not drive; having no experience driving in the snow, and afraid to navigate the many one-way streets. So I left the driving to Dennis. But soon, it became apparent that I would have to return to work, to contribute to our income. So I looked into the hospices in town, and there were two. The first I tried was happy to hire me, but did not have the hours I needed, so I went to the larger hospice. I was concerned that it may be too corporate, and not like the close-knit hospice family I came from in my home state. But I found that this hospice was everything I had hoped for! They were friendly, encouraging and supportive. They also had a large enough staff base, that the hospice teams were well supported. I had been led to the right place.

I always enjoyed caring for folks from different cultures in my home state, so I was tickled to have the opportunity to work with cultures that were new to me here, in our new state. I was also happy to find that the heart of hospice is the same, no matter where it was. The team I worked with here was just as loving, caring and supportive as I had hoped for. I made fast connections with the team members in our hospice. And I learned quickly how to navigate the one-way streets. With a new, inexpensive automatic four-wheel drive vehicle, I was happy to make visits out in the beautiful countryside, despite huge potholes and icy roads, there was also plenty of wildlife. I was thrilled to be driving in such magnificent surroundings. But as always, the focus for me, was the people I was called to serve.

I found that this was a place where people were not as driven to make more money, or to travel much. These were hometown people, family focused people, who for the most part, cared for their family members. I saw many more families supporting their loved ones through the dying process, than I ever did in my busy, wealth driven, home state. Often in my home state, family members lived several states away, so the patient had to hire a paid caregiver, instead of family caring for them. This was not as common here, where most folks gathered around their loved ones, each family member helping in one way or the other. I found this to be the case with other cultures, too; where the family was quick to gather and support their loved one. The more self-focused and self-driven we become, the more we lose that precious bond between ourselves and those we love. One day we may get a call, that the distant family member we loved, has passed away, and the chance to tell them how much we love them is lost. This slower paced, family focused town, was a welcomed change for me.

I CALL HER ANGEL

After a few years working in our new town, I was assigned quite a few patients with end-stage dementia, who lived in a dementia care facility. My experience with Grandma, made caring for those with dementia important to me. I became close to a few of the employees there, and learned even more about those with memory loss. They were dedicated to providing the best care possible, alleviating the concerns of loving family members, who had to make the decision to move their loved one to a facility. I understood how hard that decision was. It broke my heart, to accept that decision, made for my grandma, by my uncles. I knew what it felt like, to haunt the halls, making sure she was being well cared for. The truth is, caring for someone with dementia is so hard, and heartbreaking. Most of the family members of the patients at this facility, had to release the care of their dear one, into the hands of those skilled with that type of care. The staff tried to make their resident's lives as fulfilling and comfortable as possible. When they started declining, hospice would be contacted, and we would meet with the family and staff, as we collaborated in the care of their loved one. Dementia made it hard for the patient to communicate how they were feeling. Pain often led to agitation, or other responses indicating the presence of pain. It took keen observation and working with hospice team members and facility staff to keep the patients comfortable.

As they declined, communication became more difficult, and they slept more. It often seemed as if they were in their own world, and unreachable. But they were more aware than we imagined. We would often be amazed, that despite their apparent lack of awareness, they would often wait for a certain loved one to come, before they let go and passed on. What a wonderful way to know how much you meant to your loved one. Knowing they would not leave, until they knew you were there.

There was an angel who worked at this facility, who had an innate ability to know what these folks needed most, as death was approaching. I will just call her, Angel. She was a cheerful servant, and so wise with a caring heart. She came to know each of the residents there, better than just friends, and they all loved and trusted her. Her kind patience, brought the life and voices out of even the most non-responsive folks. She knew what a gift music was to them. She always asked family members what the resident's favorite music was, and made sure they had a source of that music handy. Music alone, can bring back the voice of those who had long forgotten how to speak. A favorite song, could awaken the words in their memories, and they would sing along! What a blessing that was for all who knew and loved them. Their favorite music was something she made sure was softly playing as they began to slip away. I was so thankful for her skilled observations, as she picked up on subtle changes, indicating that a resident was declining, and might need more frequent visits. By the time I would get there, she would have their favorite music softly playing, a soothing scent in the air, their favorite comfort items, and they would be cozy and quite peaceful. Not all facilities have an angel like her. I was blessed to be assigned to the facility where she worked, and gave her loving care to the people there. She told me about one of the dear ladies she cared for, as she was declining.

This lady had not spoken for years. Her daughter visited her faithfully every day, reading to her and feeding her a bit of food or drink if she was able. She was declining, and Angel knew her time was approaching. She dressed her in a clean gown, and was tidying her room, leaning over next to her, when the lady clearly said, "Thank you." She was looking right at Angel, with her big blue eyes. Angel was startled, to be sure! She was very familiar with those fleeting moments of clarity, where their "window" of communication opens, and she wanted to make sure it stayed open, until the lady's daughter arrived, and she was due soon. So Angel told her she was beautiful, and that she had a very special daughter, who would be there soon. Angel stayed calm, despite wanting to tell her to please stay with us, until her daughter arrived. So Angel hummed, "The Old Wooden Cross" to her, and the lady said that was one of her favorite songs. Then her daughter arrived, and Angel met her at the door, gently telling her that her mother was awake, and led her swiftly to her mother's bedside. When her mother saw her, she said, "There's my girl!" And her daughter collapsed in the chair that Angel had wisely placed by her bed. She started talking to her mom. Angel heard her say, "I love you mama." And her mom replied, "I loved you more than you'll ever know." Angel quietly backed out of the room, and waited, pacing outside the door for about an hour. Then the door opened, and her daughter stood there, with tears in her eyes, smiling, and said, "She's gone." She told Angel that she thought she would never hear her mother's voice again.

God gave her a beautiful gift. Don't ever think a dementia patient is completely non-responsive. Always leave room in your heart for a miracle; they do happen. (Angel)

A SUDDEN END

Things in my life became increasingly difficult, after the sudden loss of my brother in a tragic accident. Just as I mentioned earlier, I was someone, who got that call, in the middle of the night, that my younger brother had died. I never got to tell him how much I loved him. I flew down right away, to help my parents through the terrible ordeal of grieving for and saying good-bye to their only son. Being focused on helping them, I acted more like a hospice nurse, instead of the sister who had lost her brother. I did not allow myself to grieve, I had to get back to work.

My ability to care for those who were dying, without being personally affected, came to an end. My shield was down. I had become so tender with every, heartbreaking passing. Especially when I was assigned to a young man, who was dying far too young. The heartbreak of his parents covered my own heart, weighing me down. I never became so close to a patient, as I did while caring for him; seeing the anguish in his parents, tangibly feeling their pain. The image of his strong father, unable to stop what was happening to his son, is still with me. I saved my tears for the car, where I wept over the tragedy of losing a child. All the while, reliving the loss my own parents experienced, when my brother died. I attended that young man's service, along with a couple of other hospice workers, feeling helpless in the face of his sweet parent's tragic loss.

My tenderness increased as I had to deal with another tragedy in my own life, as dark memories revealed an early childhood trauma. That invincible shield of protection around my heart, was now completely gone. I was as fragile as a human being could possibly be, the arrows of heartache piercing my heart, over and over again. It was a mountain I could not climb; so I leaned into the crevice, of the solid Rock, the breast of my Lord and Savior, Jesus Christ. What else could I do, but pray, and trust Him with my life? I loved my job so much! The people I served were so grateful for our hospice care. How could I leave this calling that God had given me? I didn't know what to do.

It was then, on that cold morning in November, that I parked outside the home of the dear lady, who was waiting for my visit. The morning that my career as a hospice nurse, ended abruptly. I could no longer serve as a nurse again.

It is a hard thing, when what you thought was your lifelong calling, comes to a screeching halt. The long process of recovery from my back injury, never was complete. Despite a long period of physical therapy, they said there was nothing more that could be done; my spine was too fragile for surgery. I would never be able to lift more than ten pounds. I still have to watch my body mechanics, to keep from being laid up in pain. The state wanted to retrain me for another comparable occupation, but I was already in my 60's, and that was not practical. I kept thinking, "If I'm not a nurse, what am I?"

I tried to focus on what I might be able to do, that would bring me joy, and to be of service to others. Loving weddings the way I do, I thought wedding planning might be fun and helpful. Excited at the prospect, I worked online for the better part of a year, to attain certification as a wedding planner. I was so happy to help plan a young couple's wedding, who went to our church. I did all that I could do, happily, and was thrilled with the floral arrangements I made from fresh flowers, for the bride, and the bridal party. Until the morning of the wedding, when I realized I could not lean over the tables to set up the center displays, without severe pain. I was so thankful for my husband, and the facility coordinator, who quickly took over that task, after I showed them that first table display. I was happy for the bride and groom, so I focused on taking photos and enjoying the ceremony. But my heart was broken, realizing this was not a practical answer.

Thankfully, my husband's job kept us okay, but there were so many bills, and we were trying to keep our heads above water. Ironically, I was out of state, having already agreed to help with the flowers for the wedding of my goddaughter, when I got the call. The state had settled my case, and we would be getting a monetary compensation that would cover all of our bills! I called my husband to tell him, and we rejoiced, praising God for His mercy. But then I realized that my nursing career was officially over. I was reminded quickly, that I could trust the God who carries me, and focus on being a wife, mother and grandmother, the thing I really loved most in life.

Eventually, I joined a GriefShare group, a Christian program for those who are grieving. It was a time of healing for me, spiritual healing, as I allowed myself to grieve the loss of my brother. I recommend this program to anyone who has lost a loved one, no matter how long it has been since your loss. It was three years before I made that step. It was time, and I was ready.

I brought out the wooden crosses that my brother liked to make, and had given to me, and hung them up in my home. It was a blessed reminder that he was now with the Master Carpenter in heaven. Knowing the one you love is in heaven, is the best comfort in loss. I knew my brother loved Jesus, but I also know how much the Lord loves each of us. I had seen Jesus reaching out to so many, giving them the opportunity to accept His love and forgiveness. So don't lose hope! We don't know all that happens during that time of passing.

(You can contact GriefShare at GriefShare.org where you can sign-up for a group at a church near you, or an online group. They also have a free, encouraging, daily email that you can sign-up to receive. It was a welcoming, daily message, that brought great comfort to my heart. I pray that you too, can find the comfort of Christ in your grief, and find support through GriefShare, in your journey.)

ANOTHER TYPE OF NURSING

I became more involved with our church, and one day, one of our pastors asked if I would like to join their Care Team. I wasn't sure what that was, and the pastor explained, that there were a few ladies, some were retired nurses, who met weekly to pray for the sick in our church, and to make visits to the hospital on the church's behalf. We were able to pray for those who were sick and encourage them, and also to let the pastors know just how they were doing, as a liaison for the pastors. I was so happy to serve in that way! I loved going in to pray for and read Scriptures with those in the hospital. It was a way of being a nurse in a spiritual sense. Then, with the COVID restrictions, we could no longer make those visits. Now we support them in prayer, as the body of Christ. This has been a blessing for me, to serve in prayer. I am so grateful for this time, that I have had the privilege to intercede for those who are sick, injured or dying. Then, God gave me another, more urgent calling. To write books, from my own heartaches, to comfort those who are facing similar trials and troubles. My "nursing," would not be hands on, but heart to heart. It was difficult to begin! But when I started writing, I could not stop! It just flowed out from the Spirit who strengthened me, my hands barely keeping up!

It is a blessing, to pour out your heart on paper, or the keyboard. Those things that have roughed us up in life, can be cleansed in a way, through writing them out. Those trials also have served to make us more understanding of others, more compassionate, despite the pain we experience in the moment. We are all human, we all have had our share of troubles in this life, but it is Christ in us, that leads us to reach out and help others who may be in the midst of trials. In 2 Corinthians, we are reminded,

> Blessed be the God and Father of our Lord Jesus Christ, the Father of mercies and God of all comfort, who comforts us in all our tribulation, that we may be able to comfort those who are in any trouble, with the comfort with which we ourselves are comforted by God. (2 Corinthians 1:3–4)

I WILL NOT FEAR

There were so many times, that people who were close to passing, saw Jesus at the foot of their bed, or an angel giving them the hope of heaven. God does not let any of us go, without revealing Himself to them in some way; giving them every chance to accept His free gift of life. I saw it so often, that it really increased my love and faith in His deep, everlasting love for us. If someone will not accept that love, it is not because God rejected them, but because they rejected Him. In my time as a hospice nurse, I can only recall less than five people, who I knew had rejected Him, and would not see the light of heaven, but only the darkness and pain of eternity without Him. We who have accepted the free gift of eternal life through Jesus Christ our Lord, have no need to fear the death of our mortal bodies. If we love Him, we should long to be with Him, in His timing. There is a time for death, for each of us, but only the Lord knows when that will be. We do not fear that glorious regeneration. When we receive new, heavenly bodies, without pain, without sickness, in the perfection of His creation. Eternal bodies, to live and serve our Lord in heaven. What a glorious promise of God!

> And God will wipe away every tear from their eyes; there shall be no more death, nor sorrow, nor crying. There shall be no more pain, for the former things have passed away. (Revelation 21:4)

Some do not realize what awaits them! I know of true believers, who still fear death. Some have held the belief, that if God loved them, He would not let them die. This is not true; God's love does not end when we leave our earthly bodies, it has only just begun!

Sometimes, God heals us by giving us a new body, in heaven, with Him. A body that will never be sick or know pain, a body that will live forever in the kingdom of God! What a wonderful thing to look forward to. I look forward to my new body! My sun damaged skin requires routine checks for skin cancers, and I have had three removed already. I can't wait to see the new skin I will have in heaven. I may not have freckles there; because there will be no more sun. Jesus Christ will be our light, and there will be no darkness. I have a back injury that limits what I can do physically, but all pain will be gone in heaven. How I look forward to eternity with my Lord! I only trust that I will not leave this earth, until I have used all that He has given me to serve Him here. When my time does come, I will be like a kid with a ticket to Disneyland, eagerly waiting for the doors to open. Our "ticket," is our faith in the Lord Jesus, who paid the price for all of our sins, by His death on the cross. Then He conquered sin and death, by rising again the third day, in victory over the enemy. Soon, He will come again, to receive us up to Himself, judging those who reject Him, and creating a new heaven and a new earth. (See Revelation chapter 21)

The Lord Jesus could return at any time! We must use all that He has given us, to share His love and salvation to all we can, while we can. The time is short.

> And do this, knowing the time, that now it is high time to awake out of sleep; for now our salvation is nearer than when we first believed. (Romans 13:11)

Indeed! The time is so close! It is hard not to see all of the signs that are accumulating before our very eyes! We must not ignore what the Lord is revealing to us. Read with me, in 1 Thessalonians 5, with the fresh eyes of today, and all we see happening around us.

> But you, brethren, are not in darkness, so that this Day should overtake you as a thief. You are all sons of light and sons of the day. We are not of the night nor of darkness. Therefore let us not sleep, as others do, but let us watch and be sober. For those who sleep, sleep at night, and those who get drunk are drunk at night. But let us who are of the day be sober, putting on the breastplate of faith and love, and as a helmet the hope of salvation. For God did not appoint us to wrath, but to obtain salvation through our Lord

Jesus Christ, who died for us, that whether we wake or sleep, we should live together with Him.

Therefore comfort each other and edify one another, just as you also are doing. (1 Thessalonians 5:4–11)

Oh, just think of it! Our Lord and Savior Jesus, could arrive at any moment! My heart just thrills within me! How can we think of anything else? Our Lord is at the door! Why do we busy ourselves with useless things, that have no eternal weight in the kingdom of God? The gifts of the Holy Spirit, within you, given to you to be used for His glory; are you using them for your Lord? Are we so blinded by the useless pursuits of this world, that we have lost sight of the purpose for which our Lord of Glory created us? Can we not see that He, our Savior King, is coming soon to us in the clouds of heaven? Oh, don't you want Him to snatch you up with Him, to live forever with Him? I know I do! The line from the verses above, that speaks so clearly to me, is the end of verse 8, "And as a helmet the hope of salvation." I want to wear the shining helmet of my hope for His salvation! I want all to see that we do have hope! And that our hope is in the Lord Jesus Christ, our Savior, and our King!

While the world spins out of control, with heartache, disease, plaques and natural disasters all around us, we need to be shining beacons of the hope we have through Christ Jesus. Jesus has called us above all, to have love for one another. (1 John 4:7) How can we love others, if we keep the truth of the saving grace of Jesus Christ to ourselves? If the Lord is not willing that any should perish, how can we allow those around us to slip away into the darkness, without reaching out with the light of Christ? Is this not what we were created for?

I pray that when our Lord returns, every one of us who calls themselves Christ's, would be found by Him in service to Him, when that trumpet sounds! Oh, to be called up to glory with Him!

BEYOND THE GATES

I had a beautiful dream! I was running up a beautiful, country road; the sky was glowing yellow and pink, as if it was close to sunset. The fields around me were green and golden, with high grasses waving in the wind. And then, as I approached the top of the hill, I saw something bright, off to my right in the sky. It was far off, but close enough for me to see it clearly. It was Jesus! He was standing in what appeared to be an open doorway, with golden light shining out around Him! I ran towards Him, through the field, lifting my arms up to Him, crying out, "Jesus! Jesus!" And he reached out, and took me up with him.

As I woke up, the verse that came to mind, was, "Behold, I am near, at the door!" (Matthew 24:33, Mark 13:29) In the Scriptures, the fields often represent the world; and the high grasses, could be wheat, ripe for harvest. Sunset was approaching, the end is near!

I also noticed that the sun was setting to my left, and the sky to my right, was the deep blue of approaching night. It made the brightness of that doorway stand out like daylight, as I looked and saw Jesus, coming for me. This verse came to mind.

> For as the lightning comes from the east and flashes to the west, so also will the coming of the Son of Man be. (Matthew 24:27)

I had another dream, several months later. It was brief, but visually beautiful. It was a woman, dressed in a flowing, white gown. She had long, golden hair, blowing gently with the wind, as she stood on the top of a grassy hill. In her hand, she held a long silver cord between her fingertips. She turned, and smiled at me, and it seemed that she was about to release the silver cord, as it waved in the wind, barely secure between her two fingertips. I awoke, wondering about the "silver cord," knowing it was in the Scriptures, but not sure where. I was eager to look it up, and found it, in Ecclesiastes.

> Remember your Creator before the silver cord is loosed,
> Or the golden bowl is broken,
> Or the pitcher shattered at the fountain,
> Or the wheel broken at the well.
> Then the dust will return to the earth as it was,
> And the spirit will return to God who gave it.
> (Ecclesiastes 12:6–7)

Then a few months later, another dream, or dreams. They were so brief, like glimpses into heaven. First, I saw a golden, gilded, ornate fence, covered to overflowing with large purple grapes with big, bright green leaves. There was a golden domed gazebo, near the fence, in the distance. I closed my eyes, and when I opened them, I was in the gazebo, and saw a large, shallow, wooden bowl, filled up to around the edges with grain that was ground, as a glistening, golden stream of oil was being poured into the grain in the middle of the bowl.

When I woke up, I was pondering on those beautiful images, wondering about them, when suddenly, the words of an old hymn came to my lips! It is based on a verse in Jeremiah 31.

> Therefore, they shall come and sing in the height of Zion,
> And shall flow together to the goodness of the LORD,
> For wheat, and for wine, and for oil, and for the young,
> For the young of the flock and of the herd:
> And their soul shall be as a watered garden;
> And they shall not sorrow any more at all.
> (Jeremiah 31:12, King James Version)

Oh! Just think of it! To be forever with our Lord and King. To see the crystal clear, streets of gold, so pure, they're transparent! To sing with the heavenly host, praises to our King! Throwing down our crowns before Him, in adoration and heart-felt devotion, to the One who shed His precious blood for us!

This is the culmination of all we were created for! To be dwelling forever with the One who loved us so, that He gave His One and Only Son, the Lord Jesus Christ, as an offering, to wipe out the debt of sin against us, forever, for those who love Him.

It may not be today, or tomorrow. It may come unexpectantly for some of us, or we may live to see that Day, when Jesus comes for us all, His bride, His beloved ones. However that day comes, I am so eager and ready! I pray you are too! I trust that you are wearing your shining helmet of the hope of salvation. I pray that the hope of heaven shines so brightly in you, that all who see you, will be drawn to our Lord and Savior, Jesus Christ.

God bless each of you, as you seek to serve Him all your days. In His love, Denise Parker

BIBLIOGRAPHY

Wellman, Sam "Florence Nightingale: Lady with the Lamp." Heroes of the Faith series, Barbour Publishing Inc. 1999